Praise for *Desperately Seeking Parents*

"Take heed, you and your child are in good hands with the advice that rests between the pages of this wonderful book. Thank the good Lord that there is a writer with the scholarship and good sense to write a book that parents can safely rely on."

—David Stein, Ph.D.
author of *Unraveling the ADD/ADHD Fiasco*
and *Ritalin is Not the Answer*

"If every parent read this book and incorporated Dr. Paterno's principles and techniques, every pediatrician's office would see far fewer children with behavior problems."

—Colette Sabbagh, M.D.
Pediatrician, Bangor, Maine

"Dr. Paterno has managed to squeeze 3,000 years of common sense and experience, a command of child development and behavioral theory, tons of wit and humor, and dozens of practical solutions into this thoroughly readable parenting guide."

—Toby Tyler Watson, Psy.D.
Executive Director
International Center for the Study of Psychiatry & Psychology

Dathan Paterno's book, *Desperately Seeking Parents*, directly addresses the single most important aspect of parenting and family life--the exercise of proper parental authority. The failure to exert rational, loving parental authority is the single greatest cause of disturbed and disturbing behavior among our children.

Read this book and you will improve your parenting! Parents who take this book to heart and apply its principles will quickly find that their children become more self-disciplined and happier. Instead of an "ADHD kid" or a "Bipolar child" who supposedly needs medication, you will find yourself living with a self-disciplined and caring youngster who needs nothing more than skilled parenting and good schooling.

—Peter R. Breggin, M.D.
Psychiatrist, Ithaca, NY
and author of *The Ritalin Fact Book* and *Reclaiming Our Children*.

DESPERATELY SEEKING PARENTS

Why Your Child Needs a Parent in Charge & How to Become One

DATHAN A. PATERNO, Psy.D.

WestBow
PRESS

WestBow Press™
1663 Liberty Drive
Bloomington, IN 47403
www.westbowpress.com
Phone: 1-866-928-1240

First published by WestBow Press: 1/15/2010

ISBN: 978-1-4497-0017-1 (sc)
ISBN: 978-1-4497-0018-8 (hc)
ISBN: 978-1-4497-0016-4 (e)

Library of Congress Control Number: 2010920066

Printed in the United States of America
Bloomington, Indiana

This book is printed on acid-free paper.

Parenting Assessment

Assess your parenting style and family hierarchy by circling the response that most accurately reflects your experience with your child(ren).

1. **My children boss me or tell me what to do.**
   A. Often
   B. Sometimes
   C. Are you kidding? My kids would never dream of ordering me around!

2. **If I say no to something, my child will go to my spouse or another adult to get what he or she wants.**
   A. Often
   B. Sometimes
   C. Are you kidding? My kid would never dream of answer shopping!

3. **When I say no to my child, I get eye-rolling, arm-folding, stomping, door-slamming, and a series of looks as if I'm from another planet.**
   A. Often
   B. Sometimes
   C. Are you kidding? My kid would never dream of disrespecting me like that!

4. **My child says things like "whatever" or whispers things under his or her breath to or about me.**
   A. Often
   B. Sometimes
   C. Are you kidding? My child knows better than to do that.

5. **My children whine, beg, and plead to get what they want.**
   A. Often
   B. Sometimes
   C. Are you kidding? My children know that "Please, may I..." is the *only* way to get what they want.

6. **My child insults me or calls me "lame," "retarded," "backward," or other names.**
    A. Often
    B. Sometimes
    C. Are you kidding? My kid wouldn't dare insult me!

7. **My children complain of boredom; I have to make sure they are entertained.**
    A. Often
    B. Sometimes
    C. Are you kidding? My kids know that I will assign them a list of chores a mile long if they complain of being bored. They keep themselves occupied independently.

8. **My children's behavior is intolerable at restaurants or other public places to the point where I cannot take them anywhere decent behavior is expected.**
    A. Often
    B. Sometimes
    C. Are you kidding? My kids know that they will be eating nothing but wheat bread and broccoli if they act out in public!

9. **When other children misbehave in my home, I feel powerless to intervene or discipline them.**
    A. Often
    B. Sometimes
    C. Are you kidding? Any child who comes to my home must follow my rules; if he refuses   to accept my rules or discipline, he will leave and not return until that changes.

10. **My children do not seem to care what I think of their behavior, so I do not acknowledge, praise, respect, or show appreciation for positive behavior.**
    A. Often
    B. Sometimes
    C. Are you kidding? My children and I thrive on mutual gratitude and expression of affection, especially when they behave well!

If you circled "C" on all (or almost all) 10 items, congratulations! You are a **Parent in Charge**. Of course, you can always learn how to more securely maintain a proper family hierarchy and manage your children, but you are on the right track.

If you circled "A" or "B" on multiple items, you are a more **Submissive Parent**. If you read and utilize the principles and techniques in this book, however, you can become a **Parent in Charge**.

Read on!

Foreword

By Dr. David Stein

The mark of a good writer is that he is clear and easy to understand; this applies to books from chemistry to philosophy. The mark of a great writer is that he can take complex ideas and make them seem simple. Dr. Dathan Paterno achieves both. When I first read this manuscript, I could not put it down. Dr. Paterno uses his quick wit and warmth to create a book that is fun to read, easy to follow, and yet is deceptive because to the trained eye, it is apparent that deep scholarship underlies what he writes.

I have read many, many parenting books. Most of them are filled with rubbish and not worth the paper they are printed on. These books are detrimental to the welfare of our children. They promote permissive parenting, which was popularized in the 1950s by Dr. Benjamin Spock. Before he died, Dr. Spock admitted that he had made a huge mistake and expressed a wish that he should have stayed with pediatrics and not ventured into the world of pop child psychology. Other books are filled with psychobabble, making claims that we should never discipline children because it would ruin their psyche and self-esteem. In fact, it is *not* disciplining them that will end up ruining their psyche. Furthermore, almost all the parenting books out there, even the ones for children with so-called special needs, such as Attention-Deficit/ Hyperactive Disorder, violate the most solid and basic principles of good psychology. Theoretically, these parenting methods *should not work*, and realistically, they *do not work*.

This book by Dr. Paterno is rock solid. His underlying philosophy— that it is our responsibility to mold our children's behaviors and beliefs—is right on the money. God gave us this charge and it is our job to honor it. Too many children are out of control monsters. It seems to be politically correct to blame their misbehaviors on a wide variety of make-believe mental diseases, for which not one shred of plausible or ethical evidence exists. I repeat, not one shred of evidence exists.

Dr. Paterno ascribes part of the problem directly to the real cause(s) of problem behaviors: a permissive philosophy and confused, muddled parenting. We agree that this is not the parents' fault. Rather, the pop psychologists and psychiatrists confuse parents with their harebrained ideas. Well folks, here is a book that combats this trend. This is the stuff of good *and* great writing. In-depth scholarship underlies every word written here by Dr. Paterno, and his writing will make it difficult for the reader to put it down.

This book is not only filled with healthy and solid philosophy about children and family, but Dr. Paterno offers specific steps to achieve the kind of family many parents desire deep in their hearts. He enumerates the things parents need to do, but he goes even further: he gives guidelines for implementation, i.e., how to get the job done. I think his idea of the Family Constitution is fantastic. This is both a *learn* and a *do* book.

I love his section on how to be a lousy parent. This is an excellent paradoxical ploy to make us pay attention to ourselves. It will make you think.

Dr. Paterno courageously takes on the issue of spanking. I agree with his position; I think you will too, partly because he is not an extremist on this inflammatory issue. Pay close attention to what he has to say, because he says it well and he is *right on*.

I've known Dr. Paterno for many years. I would never consider reviewing a manuscript unless I *know* that the author is 100 percent ethical and 1,000 percent knowledgeable. I was eager to read this manuscript, but I was surprised at Dr. Paterno's mastery for writing. The reader, I can promise, will say that it is as if the author were in the room chatting with you.

One might be tempted to say that the writer simply has good common sense. He does, but that is not the essence of this book. What seems like common sense is actually a deep grasp of the scholarship of child psychology.

Dr. Paterno will disarm you. His presentation might tempt the reader to say, "Well, it's only good common sense." His knowledge of children and family is the product of a clear thinker who has spent years filtering through the literature of psychology and philosophy. No one could produce a work as good as this without such devoted study. Therefore, reader, take heed, you and your child are in good hands with the advice that rests between the pages of this wonderful book.

Thank the good Lord that there is a writer with the scholarship, the good sense, and the ethics to write a book that parents can safely rely on.

David B. Stein, Ph.D.
Professor of Psychology and Criminal Justice
Virginia State University

Acknowledgments

It would be tempting to disregard these acknowledgment pages as silly. Part of me is inclined to say that I wrote this book completely on my own—that I prospected and mined all of the ideas and that nobody helped me at all with the writing, editing, publishing, marketing, and printing. Of course, that would be a lie.

First, I thank God for guiding me through my education—both formal and informal. Thankfully, He shepherded me into personal and professional relationships with some of the most learned and richest minds in the field. Second, I thank my wife for her undying support and unwavering encouragement to finish this book so that I can make some money and pay off my student loans, so, in turn, she can finally get the new house she's been bugging me about for the last three years. You're a piece of work, woman.

Next, I acknowledge my family of psychologists (my wife, mother, step-father, and mother-in-law), who have encouraged my crazy ideas about family. I shout a special "huzzah" to my parents, mainly for gently informing me in my twenties that I would never write the great American novel and that I'd better get off my duff and get a real degree so I can afford their nursing home when they get old.

I am compelled to thank Dr. John Timmerman of Calvin College. This gem of a teacher allowed me into his super exclusive Advanced Creative Writing class (after I agreed to buy a pair of Birkenstocks and committed to writing at least one ode to an oak tree). What he received in return was a measure and style of prose that probably nauseated him and cast doubt on the wisdom of his decision. Yet he also encouraged me to find my writing voice—however obnoxious that voice proved to be—and helped me hone my satirical nature into the shimmering bayonet that I have liberally wielded on some psychiatrists and ex-girlfriends. Dr. Timmerman, you have my profound thanks.

I thank Dr. Eliezer Schwartz of the Illinois School of Professional Psychology in Chicago for his clinical acumen and deep wisdom. I thank my former colleagues at the Arlington Center—especially Dan Goff, Psy.D. and Bradley Olson, Psy.D., M.Div.—for taking me on as an intern, even though you "weren't taking on interns." As if you could say no to me …

I would be remiss if I neglected to highlight Dr. David Stein's profound influence in my thinking about children and diagnosis, as well as his focus on equipping parents rather than fixing broken children. *Ritalin Is Not the Answer* compelled me to perceive struggling children from a completely different perspective. His obliging support and critical input with this book has been invaluable. Many of the techniques expressed in this book sprung from his original ideas on parent-based interventions.

I thank all the professionals at WestBow Press for believing in me and in these ideas. Specifically, I owe a debt of gratitude to my editor, Joseph J. Satton, who helped transform this raw material into something comprehensible and, hopefully, palatable. I also thank my friends Steve Engel, James Falzone, Mark Lundell, and Troy McLennan; I have treasured their collective wisdom and friendship for decades. I thank my children for proving that normal and wonderful children are often silly, selfish, and ridiculous. Every day, you remind me of the huge returns that come from investing in such great kids.

Finally, I thank all my clients—past, present, and future—for getting better in spite of me and for being my therapeutic guinea pigs while I developed these ideas and discovered my own personal sense of a therapeutic self.

Table of Contents

Introduction

The voice of parents is the voice of gods,
for to their children they are heaven's lieutenants.

~William Shakespeare

They should rule who are able to rule best.

~Aristotle

1

Little Jimmy

Eight-year-old Jimmy threw a major league, YouTube-worthy tantrum when he noticed his mother Laura stuffing towels and sunscreen into her pool bag. It was one of those glorious days, perfect for lying out at the pool: sunny but not too hot. Two of her girlfriends were joining them, along with their kids.

Jimmy had other plans. "I don't want to go to the pool! I'm not going! I want to play my Wii!" Mom reasoned and pleaded with her son, to no avail. Within seconds, he was grimacing, shrieking, and flailing his body around like a tornado. In the midst of it all, his fists of fury knocked over a valuable picture frame, cracking both the glass and the frame.

No threat or bribery seemed to persuade or calm him. Although a part of Laura wanted to wring his neck, she found herself calling her girlfriend. "I'm sorry, I can't make it; Jimmy really doesn't want to go." As soon as those words hit Jimmy's ears, the tornado dissipated and his disposition calmed. At least she got some laundry done while he happily gorged himself on video games.

There are two types of parents. Those of you who can relate to Laura fit the first type: the *submissive (wimpy) parent.* Jimmy's attitude, sense of entitlement, and out-of-control behavior tend to befuddle these parents. Today, many parents feel a similar desperation and powerlessness in their relationships with their children; they sheepishly allow such outlandish behavior. I hear more and more parents complain that establishing and maintaining order, peace, and loving relationships in their family has somehow escaped them. Their hope ebbs and flows as they watch the parade of experts on *Dr. Phil* and *Supernanny,* hoping to find the magic words or parenting techniques that will finally turn their family into the Brady Bunch they always dreamed it would be.

The other type of parent is the *Parent in Charge.* Parents in Charge read about Jimmy and Laura and confidently say to themselves, "That would never happen in my home." I am a Parent in Charge. Jimmy 'o the Tantrum wouldn't last five minutes in my home. First, I would never allow him to have a tantrum at his age; second, if he did, he would quickly wish he hadn't. Parents in Charge do not tolerate nonsensical behavior because they recognize that they are the boss, they are the ones in control, and they can demand superb behavior from their children. Period.

Why I Wrote this Book

Children desperately need Parents in Charge. First and foremost, this book will convince you why Parents in Charge provide the best template for their children and the best chance of the children becoming successful in their future relationships and career. It shows how Parents in Charge will discover harmony in their marriages and a greater sanity and sense of self-respect.

The next section shows you a simple, organized, sensible, natural, and highly effective way to establish yourself as a Parent in Charge. After reading this section, you will differentiate between your children's rights and the privileges that they must earn. You will also simplify all of your rules and expectations into a far simpler structure called the Four Expectations.

The book then provides a complete but simple structure for the change your family will experience, called your Family Constitution. I show you how to write your own and give an example of a highly successful Family Constitution. You will learn how to implement this constitution, including appropriate rewards and consequences that are consistent with your child's needs and your position as the Parent in Charge.

Finally, the book tackles several difficult parenting issues, such as how to be a single Parent in Charge, whether to spank, reasonable limits for modern media (such as Internet use, cell phones, video games), and how to deal with children with unique personalities and needs.

I have worked with children and their parents for more than eighteen years in psychiatric hospitals, in therapeutic day schools, and in my own private psychology practice. I have seen countless families who, for some reason, have lost their sense of unity. Sensing their family crumbling, parents cling to whatever shred of dignity they can muster. They come to me for advice, for hope, for solutions—anything I can offer them that might help them recapture their vision of family and relationship.

How This Book Is Unique

Dozens of parenting books line the shelves at local libraries and bookstores, offering a broad range of parenting philosophies and approaches. Which is best? Which offers the most realistic, time-tested approach to parenting? The number of choices can be bewildering and depressing. Some instruct you to count to three. Some tell you to give your child choices. Some insist that diagnoses like Attention-Deficit/Hyperactive Disorder (ADHD), Oppositional Defiant disorder (ODD), Developmental Disorder, LBD (the dreaded Lazy Butt Disorder) should reduce your expectations for your child. Still others insist that children have rights that are equal to parents—that parents do not have the right to be in control of their children.

Baloney! You are the parent! You are in charge. You *must* be in charge. Your child *needs* you to be in charge, in control, the boss. This book pulls no punches. Call me a throwback, an old-fashioned conservative. Fine. I know what works. I have seen it in my own home and with countless families. Children are desperately seeking Parents in Charge.

Almost every family I encounter whose union is broken struggles with establishing and maintaining a proper hierarchy, where adult authority and expectations are primary and the children's desires come second. Time after time, exhausted and despondent parents tell me that their child does as he pleases and that nothing they do as parents has any meaningful or lasting effect. They feel stuck.

Some do not perceive their family hierarchy as broken or dysfunctional. They have bought into the idea that their number-one priority as parents is to satisfy the desires of their children in order to show their love and maintain peace and order. Others recognize the brokenness in their family hierarchy but do not quite know what to do about it. Many parents who come to me in crisis doubt whether they can ever regain some semblance of harmony in their family.

I wrote this book primarily for two kinds of parents. First, those parents who recognize their broken family structure and realize they must reestablish a proper hierarchy in their family. For them, this book will equip them to reestablish a semblance of control, regardless of what they have done or not done to lose it. Second, this book challenges those who do not yet recognize what has happened in their family or in the culture of families today. For them, this book constitutes a wake-up call. My message is clear: if you do not establish or maintain a proper familial hierarchy, you will not only reap sorry benefits in the future, but you will fail to provide one of your child's most basic needs.

Additionally, this book provides a foundation for new parents. For them, this book provides a framework for parenting, so that both parents can enter into the joys and trials of parenting with a solid philosophical underpinning and a simple, flexible game plan for how to establish and maintain a healthy hierarchy in the family. This will reap great rewards in both the short and long term for them and their children.

Someone's Going to Lead Your Family

The question of hierarchy in the family is not whether someone should be in charge of your family. The question is *who* will be in charge of your family. The truth is, someone will lead and take control of your family. That someone will assert power and dominance, either through legitimate means or by waging guerrilla warfare through misbehavior, disrespect, demands, and scare tactics. Many of you parents know exactly what I mean.

So, why would parents reject the idea that they should be in charge? Why in the world would otherwise intelligent and educated adults give up the reins of their home and allow their children to rule the roost? At first glance, it might be tempting to judge these wimpy parents; who hasn't been in public and thought, *Why do they let their kid behave like that?* However, judgment does not equip parents to change. The more I work with parents, the more I am convinced there are several understandable reasons why some struggle with this.

Some do so because of philosophical reasons. Because they revere the concept of democracy, they figure that families should function democratically. In this setup, all family members have equal power and say-so: there are no generals, majors, or grunts. Nice idea, and I'm sure it works for some families; there are always exceptions to the rule. It just doesn't work for most families.

Others simply neglect to think ahead. They enter parenting without explicitly specifying their beliefs about family structure, so they never consciously establish a hierarchy. The usual consequence here is that the children, because they are bright, sense a power vacuum. Because they are human, they eagerly and deftly fill that vacuum. That's what normal children do; it's not their fault. Years later, these parents ponder how they lost control of the family when they truly never had it in the first place.

When a family does not establish a proper hierarchy—with parents in charge and children submitting to their parents' authority—a family runs quite poorly, if at all. Most children are unable to make consistently solid and wise decisions for themselves. If they could, they would be living on their own and taking care of themselves. They wouldn't need parents at all! Parents in Charge know that children rarely have the knowledge, common sense, sense of responsibility, and ingenuity to lead themselves. As a result, the Parent in Charge establishes control early in a child's life.

In Control versus Controlling

Okay, some of you might be thinking that I am a power-hungry control freak. Nothing could be further from the truth. I have better things to do than micromanage my children. I want to give them tons of freedom—as long as they earn it and they prove they can handle it. At the same time, I strongly believe that children need a strong leader at the helm, until they can safely and responsibly control the rudder of their own lives.

Let me make clear what I mean by phrases like "hierarchy," "the boss," "in charge," "in control," and "maintain power." When I use "hierarchy" and other similar terms, I am referring to the idea of unequal *position*, not unequal *value* or *worth*. Take the school hierarchy, for example. In most schools, a teacher has a higher position than that of the students. This does not mean that she is better, more valuable, or necessarily smarter than the student (although hopefully she knows more). For logical and practical reasons, she holds a higher authority than the students do. At the same time, this does not mean that the teacher holds *absolute* authority over her students. Similarly, the principal has a higher authority than does the teacher, and so on.

Another example is the military; beginning with private first class and moving up to general and commander-in-chief, the military commissions qualified persons to maintain more power, authority, and corresponding responsibilities than those who are lower in the hierarchy. Most soldiers who are not officers would admit that they do not have the knowledge, wisdom, or experience to make crucial strategic decisions. Therefore, submitting to the authority of their superiors seems logical and self-serving. With hard work and consistent, loyal service, many soldiers earn higher ranks, which come with certain privileges, such as increased trust, freedom, respect, and responsibility.

To be *in control* of your child is not the same as *controlling* your child. Take expectations for mealtime, for example. A Parent in Charge who is *in control* tells her child that he may have dessert only if he eats two of the three helpings of food, including vegetables. This parent follows through by either allowing dessert when earned or denying dessert if not. If her child chooses to eat and gets dessert, fine; if her child chooses not to eat and therefore does not get dessert, fine. The child has chosen his consequence.

The controlling parent, on the other hand, forces her child to eat every last bite of food on his plate, whether the child is hungry or not and whether he likes the food or not. We have a name for parents who tend to deny these freedoms when their children are trustworthy, or who seem to revel in controlling all spheres of a child's life, however minute or inconsequential: *control freak*. At best, this kind of parenting squashes a child's spirit; at worst, it incites rebellion and secrecy. In contrast, the Parent in Charge often shares or relinquishes control and power when he allows certain freedoms and seeks to increase those freedoms as other family members exhibit trustworthiness.

As I mentioned, someone has to lead the family. Whether you label that leadership as "in charge" or being "the boss" or even "commander-in-chief," a healthy family has an authority who serves and commands respect from those who submit to the parental leadership and position.

Where Does Parental Authority Come From?

So who says that there should be a family hierarchy and that parents should be the ones who hold the authority in the family? Am I just spouting my own subjective view of family? Am I just a power-hungry grown-up who wants to place children under the collective parental thumb? I think not.

Three compelling and authoritative sources grant parents full authority over their children. These sources have *commissioned* parents to establish themselves as the head of the family hierarchy. These are God, the government, and common sense.

God

Most of the world's religions expressly command a family hierarchy, with parents in charge. The three largest religions in the Western Hemisphere—Christianity, Judaism, and Islam—all have specific dictums that support parents' position of authority in the family. The most well-known comes from the Judeo-Christian Scriptures. The Bible includes the Fifth Commandment: "Honor your father and your mother" (Exodus 20:12). The command is not only given as an imperative, it also comes with a reason: "that you may live long in the land." God promises great reward for children who submit to his prescribed hierarchy.

The Christian Scriptures also warn children not to defy their parents: "All who curse father or mother shall be put to death; having cursed father or mother, their blood is upon them" (Leviticus 20:9). Yikes. As if that warning weren't enough, the Bible includes this stern warning to parents:

> If someone has a stubborn and rebellious son who will not obey his father and mother, who does not heed them when they discipline him, then his father and his mother shall take hold of him and bring him out to the elders of his town…. Then all the men of the town shall stone him to death. So you shall purge the evil from your midst; and all Israel will hear, and be afraid. (Deuteronomy 21:18–21)

Now, before you brand me a child-hater or conclude I am recommending you stone your child, please know that I am not suggesting anything of the sort.[1] I am simply showing how clear the

---

1   I have, on the other hand, worked with some parents who have *wanted* to stone their children, and after hearing their plight and meeting their progeny, I couldn't blame them.

Christian Scriptures are on the family hierarchy and the importance of children giving parents proper respect and obedience.

Catholic and Protestant thinkers have traditionally supported a family hierarchy with parents in charge. Benedictine thought has stressed the foundation and stability provided by basic family structure; those families who ignore this risk their children rejecting all standards of behavior: "Their law is what they like to do, whatever strikes their fancy." (*The Rule of St. Benedict*, p. 1)

The Protestant Puritans have been quite direct in their parenting guidelines. Dr. C. Matthew McMahon pulls no punches when describing proper family hierarchy:

> Children are not to run the household. Parents run the household. Parents do not cater to their children, they take care of their children. There is a huge difference between the two.... God has placed parents over children. Never, ever, should children have authority over parents in any way, shape, or form. If they do, then the family is dysfunctional. (*How Not to Foul up the Discipline of Your Children and Save Their Souls From Hell*)

The Jewish Torah—overlapping with the first five books of the Christian Bible—includes the same commands and warnings. Just as many Christian authors have further specified the family hierarchy, many Jewish teachers have supported the idea that parents must be in charge. Rabbi Shmuley Boteach explains in *Judaism for Everyone,* "there must be an authoritarian figure, usually a man, who disciplines the child when he or she does wrong and rewards him or her when he or she does right." Lest we conclude that the whole emphasis is on discipline, his admonition comes with an important caveat: "but endless discipline will ruin a child and undermine his or her self-confidence."

The Koran teaches reverence for parents as well: "We enjoined man to show kindness to his parents, for with much pain his mother bears him" (31:14) and "But he that rebukes his parents ... shall justly deserve the fate of bygone nations of men and jinn: he shall assuredly be lost." (46:18)

Clearly, religious thought supports a family hierarchy where loving, firm parents are in charge and children submit to their parents.

Government

The United States government has both implicitly and explicitly presumed parents' authority over their children. While our nation's constitution includes little to explicitly support parental rights, it does offer several rights (such as the right to vote) exclusively to adults. Furthermore, any understanding of federal and state law reveals that parents have far more rights than their children: adults can choose whether or not to go to school, buy firearms, consume alcohol (provided they are twenty-one years of age), travel wherever they would like, live where they wish, legally go to R-rated movies, and so on. They are also afforded more rights in their relationships with their children. They can choose where their family lives, decide what food and clothes to buy, choose what schools their children will attend, and make myriad choices for the family and specifically for the child.

Several decisions by the U.S. Supreme Court have explicitly supported the rights of parents to direct the upbringing of their children. Two important decisions, *Meyer v. Nebraska* and *Pierce v. Society of Sisters*, held that parenting is a fundamental constitutional right, the latter stressing parenting as among "the basic civil rights of man." In 1925, the Court underscored the parent's duty to prepare his or her child for life: "those who nurture him and direct his destiny have the right, coupled with the high duty, to recognize and prepare him for additional obligations." More recently, the Court insisted that "the interest of parents in their relationship with their children is sufficiently fundamental to come within the finite class of liberty interests protected by the Fourteenth Amendment."

Common Sense

Finally, common sense and logic both support a family hierarchy with parents in charge and children in submission to their parents. A simple logical argument should suffice:

1. In any relationship, the one who possesses superior knowledge, wisdom, and experience should be the leader and should hold a position of greater authority.
2. In most families, the parents possess superior knowledge, wisdom, and experience.

11

3.   Therefore, parents should be the leaders and hold the position of authority in the family.

Let me attempt another argument, called the *reductio ad absurdum* argument (or, the argument from the absurd). Let us imagine for a moment a country or culture that believes children should hold the authority in the family—that parents should follow, rather than lead, their children. What do you suppose would happen in a society where this was the rule? I think that just a little imagination would (and should) strike terror into your heart.

That culture would very quickly devolve into utter chaos, anarchy, and self-destruction. Bedtimes would cease to exist; all privileges would become inalienable rights; school would be optional; vegetables would never be allowed in the house (much less on children's plates); children would get frostbite from not wearing jackets, hats, or mittens; teeth would fall out due to lack of brushing; and so on. The island in *Lord of the Flies* would look like military school in comparison. One can plainly see how ridiculous it is to suggest that children should hold a family's authority. Yet many families are inadvertently living within such an absurd framework.

In the vast majority of families, parents are the ones who hold the most knowledge, wisdom, and experience in the family.[2] Their authority does not come from nowhere. For our purposes, parental authority has been clearly established, supported, presumed, and determined by God, the government, and common sense.

---

2   I understand quite well the reality that there are parents who are so ignorant, impaired, or goofy that they should not hold any authority over a chicken sandwich, much less a child. I discuss this in greater detail in Chapter Nine.

Chapter 1
Children Ruling the Roost, Oh My!

*The thing that impresses me most about America is
the way parents obey their children.*

~King Edward VIII

*Parents often talk about the younger generation
as if they didn't have anything to do with it.*

~Haim Ginott

Defiant, Disrespectful Matthew

I could hear from Yolanda's voicemail that she was in full crisis mode. She told me in an anxious, frustrated voice that their youngest son Matthew had been sent to the principal's office for telling his fifth-grade teacher to "shut up." When I called her back, she recalled several incidents where Matthew had refused to comply with his teacher's directions. She admitted that this was a growing pattern at home and that she didn't know how things had gotten this bad.

I quickly made an appointment with Yolanda and her husband Stephen. They offered to bring the current focus of the problem, Matthew, but I declined. I was confident that their son was a normal, healthy child who, like most children I see in this situation, had adapted to a chaotic, imbalanced family structure. Trying to "fix" him directly was neither possible nor wise. Fixing the family hierarchy and raising his parents' expectations of him were the keys to success in solving Matthew's problems and harmonizing the entire family.

Stephen and Yolanda, both in their mid-forties, made a pleasant, charismatic couple. Both were casual in their demeanor and dress, but respectful and keenly attentive during our initial consultation. They were civilized people who were distraught at their son's lack of civility. I could sense in their expressions and tone that this was the first time they were treating Matthew's behavior as something of an emergency.

As they discussed Matthew and his most recent misbehavior, it certainly sounded as if their son was giving them a run for their money, with blatant disrespect at home and school. He was breaking numerous house rules and speaking defiantly toward his mother, responding to basic requests with "No" or "Why should I?" Initially, Yolanda minimized the seriousness of Matthew's defiance and disrespect, suggesting that he was stressed with school, struggling to find his place in a social network, and missing his older brother who had recently left for college. As for his school behavior, Yolanda reported that he didn't much care for his teacher's rules and her tendency to single him out for his poor effort and attitude. Although she did not say so, she seemed to imply that the teacher did not have the right to expect Matthew to follow her rules.

As time went on, I asked them to grade all of their children on the Four Expectations (listed in Chapter Three), ranging from A to F. Both parents began grading each child, starting with *Safety*. At first, there was a huge disparity between the two report cards. Stephen rated his children as failing in the *Respect* and *Obedience* categories, while Yolanda somewhat defended her children by minimizing the intensity of their disrespect and disobedience. She continued to offer excuses for them. As Stephen described several instances of defiance and disobedience, Yolanda became visibly uncomfortable. I then turned to Yolanda and asked her, "What would have happened if you had told your father to 'shut the hell up' when you were a child?"

She burst out laughing and replied as most parents do: "Oh my, I don't even want to think what they would have done. It wouldn't have been pretty, I can tell you that." Her laughter revealed her awareness of how ridiculous it is to tolerate the kind of behavior Matthew was displaying. Her laughter morphed into grave concern before she asked, "How in the world did it get this way? Where did we lose them?"

Mothers know that in most families, they absorb the lion's share of responsibility for their family's functioning and dysfunction; Yolanda's family was no different. I could tell she was feeling enormous guilt; she tended to exhibit an expression that said, "I've ruined my children forever." I reminded her that all parents are imperfect and fail their children in some way. *All* parents. We have that much influence in our children's lives. That sounds hopeless, at first glance. But if we have that much destructive power, the converse is also true: we have the power to heal, correct, realign, and teach our children properly.

Stephen confessed that he had long believed that his wife tolerated far too much disrespect from the children. Since she didn't complain and because he had presumed that she was the primary Parent in Charge, he didn't step up and intervene. I asked Yolanda if she would prefer to parent from more of a team approach; with tears welling in her eyes, she nodded and said, "I need his strength." Men, pay attention to this: mothers parent far better when you support them and play an active role. Specifically, men tend to be far better at establishing a hierarchical relationship with a child. No discipline can work without this hierarchy firmly established.

I introduced the concept of the Family Constitution, and they agreed to unite themselves as a team in reworking appropriate expectations and following through more consistently. Both parents soon recognized that Matthew wasn't the only child whose respect and obedience was sorely lacking; the more they thought about it, the more they realized that almost all of their children were lacking in some form of respect or obedience. It was as if their eyes had opened to the reality of how imbalanced their family was. They had been allowing behaviors and attitudes that were far out of line. They were now committed to recapturing their lives and their family.

How It Used to Be

"Back when I was a kid, I never would have talked to my dad like that." I hear this all the time from grandparents, parents, pediatricians, and teachers. The stereotype that old folks love to hark back to the "good old days"—when children afforded their parents respect and obeyed them without question—didn't materialize out of thin air. Older persons really do remember a time when parents were in charge. Everyone knew it, so there was little argument.

Parents were the sovereigns of their family and home. Children were held to very high standards of conduct, especially with respect toward their elders. There was little tolerance for defiance or disobedience. Films like *It's a Wonderful Life* and television shows like *Little House on the Prairie* and *Leave It to Beaver* offer great examples of how children were, by and large, respectful and obedient to their parents and other elders. Even classical literary characters known for their rebellious natures, like Tom Sawyer, were generally respectful to their elders compared to some of what today's culture reveals in film and literature.

I'm not suggesting that we should all ride a time capsule back to some idyllic 1950s family life. In some ways, families are far healthier than they used to be. For example, we not only frown on child abuse, we also shine a much brighter spotlight on it. Battered women now have some legal recourse and a greater hope for escaping torturous relationships. Fathers have, to a large degree, become more involved in their children's lives. And of course, we can enjoy movie night with our massive LCD TV, rather than a rabbit-eared, black-and-white clunker like my parents had. Surely, many aspects of family life have improved.

But somehow, somewhere, the family hierarchy—and the relationship between parent and child—changed. While this book does not aim to fully investigate all of the possible reasons for how the family structure has altered during the past few generations (we have more important work to do), there are several probable suspects.

1. Divorce

The divorce rate in the United States was generally stable prior to 1960; per capita, there were only 2.2 divorces out of every 1,000 people. When no-fault divorces became the norm beginning in 1969, the divorce rate skyrocketed for over a decade, more than doubling the rate of divorces to 5.2 per 1,000 people. During this period, the number of children living with both parents declined from 85 to 68 percent, while the proportion of children living with one parent surged from 12 to 28 percent. This surge has since receded a bit, but the divorce rate continues to be quite high. A new marriage's chance of survival is little better than a coin flip.

It does not take much of a logical leap to comprehend that parents whose marriages are divided are at a severe disadvantage when it comes to parenting (Chapter Ten includes several helpful suggestions for single or divorced parents). Divorced parents are often (not always) split on how to parent, particularly when it comes to creating and maintaining appropriate expectations and limits. These parents are often left trying to parent alone—a task little easier than trying to tie a shoe with only one hand. Furthermore, many children of divorce find their parents investing time, energy, and other resources in negotiating a divorce, working increased hours (especially divorced mothers who are forced to work after a divorce), bickering with their ex-spouse, and starting a new family. This takes crucial resources away from the already challenging difficulties of parenting.

2. Child Abuse Legislation

Clinical psychologist Matthew Johnson suggests that one major factor in particular undermined parenting beginning in the latter half of the twentieth century: child abuse laws. He suggests that while child abuse laws were important and served to curb the abuse of children through cruel and excessive discipline, it had the unintended consequence of taking power away from parents. Today, most adolescents know that if their parent hits them, they can report that parent to the state's child family services, which will hold parents accountable and possibly arrest them. This is the case even if the child has been grossly defiant, disobedient, and otherwise out of control.

Dr. Johnson makes the point that when the government took away one set of parenting tools, it neglected to replace them with another that was effective, safe, and legal. Consequently, many children feel emboldened, perceiving that the government is on their side, rather than the side of the parents. Parents feel diminished in their ability to maintain authority when the government does not support their attempts at discipline.

3. Disunited Parents

Many separated or divorced parents manage to do a stellar job of united parenting; kudos to them. However, many parents who remain married are divided in their parenting values and expectations. Because parenting requires exceptional organization and commitment, unity between parents is essential.

Imagine getting dressed in the morning, with one hand trying to put on your shoes while the other was trying to button your shirt. Impossible! Both are important tasks, but they simply cannot be done independently. Parents in Charge work hard to coordinate their parenting, because they understand that good parenting requires a coordinated effort.

Some parents struggle with this because they simply do not plan ahead. Whether due to the excitement of having children or a general avoidance of possible marital conflict, many couples are not particularly interested in examining the likely challenges that parenting will foist upon them. These parents often wind up making crucial parenting decisions on the fly, with little or no discussion of family hierarchy or appropriate expectations for their children. When the dizzying number of parenting challenges shows up on their radar screen, they are ill-prepared to respond with united purpose and expectations. Those parents who recognize that they might differ on values and expectations and who negotiate these ahead of time are in a far better position for presenting a united parental front when these challenges inevitably arise.

Unfortunately, some parents use parenting as a weapon or as emotional leverage in their marriage. Naturally, some parents maintain different values and expectations for their children and tend to enforce limits differently. However, when one parent's values, expectations, or ability to discipline differs dramatically from the other's, the disunity can compromise the authority of both parents. While often unintentional, this seriously damages the family structure and ability to parent effectively.

One couple with two young daughters came to me with a marriage that was clearly struggling. The husband, Vince, had recently joined a law practice and worked outrageous hours. When he was home, he committed little energy to his children; he rarely played or talked with them and avoided disciplining them. His stay-at-home wife, Michelle, was disappointed and frustrated; she felt abandoned and resentful that she had to do the lion's share of discipline. She wasted no time complaining that he essentially forced her to be "the one who always says 'no,' while he lets them get away with just about whatever they want." In short order, the husband admitted the cause for his lackadaisical presence in the home: "Yeah, you certainly have no difficulty saying 'no' to me every night; I figured I'd just let you be consistent."

The cat was out of the bag. His choice to retaliate for sexual conflict by withdrawing from parenting was not helping his marriage or his children. Luckily, they both hated the conflict enough and loved each other enough to want to solve the problem. Once we addressed the complicated underlying issue, the husband had little trouble joining his wife as a Parent in Charge.

Another subset of parents simply has failed to recognize the importance of united values and expectations. Amazingly, some parents decide to offer their children a broad set of values and boundaries, expecting that their children can determine what is best for themselves. If you get nothing else from this book, please realize that this parenting philosophy is definitely crazy and very likely disastrous. If you have a thesaurus with you, you can apply all kinds of pejorative terms to this kind of nonsense. Your children need you to shepherd the development of their values, principles, and morals.

Imagine driving down a highway that has two different speed limits posted. One says SPEED LIMIT: 65, the other SPEED LIMIT: 45. Each is displayed prominently, although one might be less visible. If you liked to drive fast and didn't care about gas mileage, wouldn't you choose to acknowledge and adhere to the higher limit?

Similarly, children will always follow the *Least Restrictive Parent (LRP)*, also known as the "good cop" (or, to the other parent, "weasel"). Not surprisingly, the LRP is often the parent who seems more interested in being the child's buddy than her parent. Because of this, the *Most Restrictive Parent* (also known as the "bad cop") is often at her wit's end. This stricter, bad cop parent begins to believe that he—or more often, she—needs to be even stricter to make up for the spouse's lax attitude. In response, the more permissive parent feels a need to go easy on the children to make up for what is perceived to be a domineering, overly strict parent.

This sets up a helpless cycle, while the children learn to navigate and manipulate inconsistent expectations and boundaries. It is no wonder they have little respect for this kind of authority! Parents like this need to unite and settle on the family's set of beliefs, values, and principles, and then communicate them clearly to their children.

4. Lack of Extended Family

Remember shows like *The Waltons*? The parents were not only married and loving, they also had their children's grandparents living with them. Many episodes demonstrated how the wisdom and experience of their elders bolstered the family. Today, more young people settle far away from their parents, cutting them off from the rich and invaluable resources of extended family.

Extended families offer parents a number of crucial advantages in raising children, particularly in establishing a proper hierarchy and carrying on the knowledge of reasonable limits and expectations. First, grandparents and other extended family members provide crucial support for parents. Grandparents who offer their overworked or stressed children short respites can hardly overestimate the benefits. When grandparents have values, expectations, and limits similar to the parents, this provides an added bonus. In this scenario, the parents are validated, solidifying children's respect for their authority and an appreciation of the parents.

Grandparents, uncles, aunts, and other extended family members can be particularly effective when they verbally support the parents' choices and words. Supporting a parent's morals, rules, and limits can be incredibly helpful to parents. The value of hearing "Listen to your mother; she knows what she's talking about" can hardly be overestimated, whether it comes from the father, grandparents, or other adult family members.

Of course, the converse of this also holds true: if an extended family member's influence is mostly negative, then you might want to keep your children away from them. We all know about Grandma spoiling the children; we see their t-shirts and bumper stickers reveling in their role as spoiler. I'm not talking about Grandma sneaking a toddler a cookie or buying her granddaughter her eighty-fourth Webkinz. That kind of spoiling is relatively harmless. What truly destroys family hierarchy is when the child hears, "Oh, don't get on him for that; he needs to get out his feelings," or "It's okay, hon; Grandpa will give you a cookie later." This kind of message—countering a parent's discipline and values—is extremely destructive. Parents in Charge do not tolerate this.

One simpler advantage of extended families can be additional healthy relationships for children. This is relational platinum. Even more so, when a parent is unavailable, instead of plopping a child in front of a TV, computer, or video game system, a grandparent can fill the gap with something interactive, such as playing a board game, talking, gardening, building Legos, reading, going for a walk, or innumerable other activities.

My children's grandparents moved halfway across the United States to live near their grandchildren (not their daughter and son-in-law, mind you, but the grandchildren; not that we're bitter). They take them fishing; play cards, Scrabble, and other games with them; take them to community Bible study; and even carry some of the chauffeuring burden. The benefits these times afford our children far outweigh any spoiling that occurs when we parents aren't looking.

Earlier in this chapter, I discussed the importance of unity of purpose and expectations and the wisdom of planning ahead. Grandparents' ample supply of experience puts them in prime position to carry this wisdom. In relationships where their advice and counsel are welcome, they can encourage parents to look ahead to specific challenges of parenting. Parents would be wise to seek their counsel on parental unity, likely challenges to their authority, and how to manage difficult situations.

Finally, do not underestimate the value of cheap babysitting. If the old adage "If Mama ain't happy, ain't nobody happy" is true, then parents are greatly blessed when grandparents or aunts or uncles allow them to go out on a date or allow Mom to go shopping unencumbered. The parents will likely return home happier and eager to see the children, which bodes well for everyone. Can I get an "Amen!"?

5. Attributing Misbehavior to Disease, Disorder, or Disability

My wife and I recently took our son to the neighborhood park. Because I am a child psychologist, I cannot help but observe how other children behave with their parents. Sometimes, I pick up an interesting way of dealing with a parenting challenge. Sometimes, I witness yet another "how *not* to parent" display. On this day, a five- or six-year-old boy was feverishly digging a hole in a huge sandbox when a younger boy about half his size stepped near the hole, about four feet away. He was simply standing there, watching the elder boy digging. As if the younger child had threatened to destroy all that was good in the world, the elder boy began screaming at the smaller child, "Get away from my hole! This is MY hole!" Okay, not a big deal, we thought; the kid's chaperone will surely intervene and make peace.

Immediately, my wife and I began scanning the park for the boy's parent, presuming he or she would somehow intervene. A few seconds later, we noticed a mother on her cell phone (of course), strolling cautiously toward the boy. "Noah," she said in a mousey voice that inspired neither confidence nor respect, "why don't we let the boy play with us?" Not surprisingly, her son ignored her completely and continued to scream at the younger boy, who seemed to be wondering what on earth could be this kid's problem. The mother then completed her call, turned to the second child, and said *to the younger boy*, "He has ADD; he gets like that. Do you mind finding somewhere else to stand?"

My wife and I were dumbfounded. Besides the stupidity of trying to explain ADD to a four-year-old, this woman did both children a great injustice. She not only communicated to her own child that he cannot control his own behavior and therefore will not be held accountable for it, she also told the other boy that she will not provide justice for him. Unbelievable.

The past two decades or so have seen an explosion of diagnosing childhood behavior disorders such as ADHD, bipolar, intermittent explosive disorder, and oppositional defiant disorder. I doubt that many clinicians who support the diagnosing of misbehaving children with serious mental disorders intended that children would be held to lower standards and would be held less accountable for their actions, but it is clear that this has occurred on a massive scale. In my own practice, I have heard countless children and their parents blame "my bipolar" or "his ADD" for a host of inappropriate behaviors.

This nonsense needs to end. You won't hear what I'm about to tell you from the mainstream, because too many people's livelihoods would be threatened. But it's true: every one of the aforementioned disorders was invented to explain uncomfortable realities in a more palatable way. Just as children hijacked the term "cooties" to reject, tease, and marginalize other children, psychiatry concocted these disorders in part to absolve parents, teachers, and society of their responsibilities in creating respectful, obedient, and attentive children.

Please believe me: I understand the temptation. Every time one of my children misbehaves, I would much rather attribute it to something or someone other than myself. I hate taking responsibility for my children's ridiculous behavior and attitudes. But there are really only a few explanations for my child's misbehavior:

1. It is natural, caused by some biological glitch (such as the popular "chemical imbalance" fantasy).
2. Whether one calls it "sin," human nature, or animal-like instinct, all children are born with selfish tendencies, which manifest over time in certain misbehaviors. Parents and culture work to correct or minimize this tendency, with some parents more successful than others.
3. It is learned and encouraged from Mom and Dad,

both directly and more indirectly from a host of other environmental influences (e.g., peers, TV, Uncle Paul).

The first explanation is pseudoscientific hogwash. The second and third are both common sense. In the end, there is no such thing as ADD/ADHD, bipolar, or oppositional defiant disorder. These are only invented medicalized descriptors for inattentive, hurting, spoiled, undermotivated, entitled, moody, bratty, and obnoxious children. More importantly, they represent adults' inability to gain reasonable control of their children.

When we ignore our responsibility as parents, we give up our power to solve the problem. We relinquish our position and our power to psychiatrists and their drugs, who cannot possibly solve the child's core problem(s). Until parents recognize that they have the power to effect positive change in their children, far more than any professional or pill, we will continue to witness our children's behavior and attitude nosedive.

This is not to say that there are no true neurological disorders that impair a child's thinking, feeling, and behavior. Down's syndrome, Fragile X syndrome, and Huntington's disease are examples of true biological disorders; we actually have biological evidence of the disorders. Seizure disorders and several thyroid disorders also have biological markers. These disorders exist in reality and are not a result of parental failings. In contrast, there are no chemical, macroscopic, or microscopic abnormalities in children diagnosed with ADHD, bipolar, or ODD, no matter what you hear in the popular media.

While autism and autistic spectrum disorders such as Asperger's syndrome have no known biological markers as of yet, my hunch is that these are biologically caused neurological disorders and not at all caused by inadequate or wimpy parenting.

Some would protest that I am blaming parents. Yeah, so? I'm a parent; I blame myself for some of my children's goofy habits. I take responsibility and act to improve my parenting. I see the results. I am far more comforted to know that while my mistakes often result in unwanted behaviors, I also possess the power—through loving discipline—to fix what I have broken. My wife and I take responsibility

25

for parenting our children; we don't relegate this duty and privilege to doctors, chemists, or our "village."

The vast majority of children, therefore, are capable of maintaining safe behavior, respecting others, obeying authorities, and performing reasonable work. The child who, by virtue of some disease, disorder, or disability, should not be held to high standards of behavior and self-control is rare indeed. I will discuss these children in Chapter Four.

6. Film and Television

I grew up watching programs like *The Waltons, Family,* and *The Cosby Show.* As mentioned earlier, these shows exhibited families that placed parents in charge. The children were by no means perfect, nor were the parents. But overall, the children from these shows were generally quite respectful to their parents, who generally held their children to high standards of behavior.

If you watch much TV these days (and current research suggests that far too many children are watching far too much TV), you can't help but notice how powerless, ignorant, and disrespected the parents are. Conversely, you see how flippant, rude, presumptuous, and demanding children and teenagers are with their parents and other adults. Likely, this represents both a reflection of a cultural shift away from parents in charge and a model for children's behavior and attitudes toward parents and other adults.

I hate to pick on particular shows, but consider how Bart Simpson speaks to his parents—not exactly the model of humility or respect you want your children to emulate. Now consider how respectable Homer Simpson is—not a model citizen, much less a model father. Children who watch characters like this cannot help but incorporate these attitudes into their own.

7. Technological Toys

I'm not that old, but when I was a young boy, we only had radio, television, and the greatest video game of all time: Pong. Admit it, you loved Pong. Yes, this was prior to Atari, Intellivision, and Nintendo. Today, we not only have infinitely more television channels, we also have myriad electronic devices that capture children's interest, passion, and attention.

Today's video games are deeply enthralling. Even the hand-held games that Nintendo DS and the PSP offer are engrossing. Kids are so attracted to them that many want to play them in the car, at the grocery store, in restaurants, at a sibling's event, and even during "play dates." These highly stimulating games are not in themselves evil. I marvel at the creativity and exciting play of these games, and I even play them myself! As with many wonderful technologies, however, there are unintended consequences.

Many children truly become addicted to these games. More specifically, they become addicted to the high level of stimulation. The more visually exciting the game, the more addictive the game can be. The problem is that the more children play these games, the more their brains *expect* this kind of stimulation; their brains become used to the high levels of visual and auditory stimuli. As time goes on, anything or anyone offering less stimulation becomes less able to capture their attention.

It's a bit like someone who is used to rich, spicy, flavorful foods. A steady diet like this will make bland, spiceless food nearly unpalatable. When a child hears something like "Johnny, you need to go brush your teeth," it will have the same non-stimulating, spiceless quality to it. That kind of sensory input simply cannot compete with the sensory input that exciting video games offer. Parents and teachers of children whose minds enjoy a steady diet of these games are at a tremendous disadvantage when it comes to their interaction with them.

A huge number of children are spending too much time playing video games. In my own practice, a good number of adolescents and young adults spend multiple hours per day playing their Wii, Xbox 360, and PlayStation 3. For some, this is *in addition* to their television viewing. Many of today's parents are actually encouraging this kind of addictive, sedentary life-style. Fears of lurking kidnappers and gang violence are very real to parents, leading them to encourage and even insist on children staying at home, where they are likely to get bored. Because bored children tend to nag and otherwise become obnoxious, many parents are relieved when their child hunkers down to a binge of video gaming.

Another sphere of technology includes cell phones, e-mail accounts, and instant messaging programs that children now use to communicate with friends and acquaintances. These wonderful technologies offer several advantages. However, they are often used with little or no adult monitoring. This kind of precocious privacy was hardly possible twenty years ago. Many of today's parents are essentially clueless as to how these things work, much less know how to monitor them. Children are able to explore a host of pseudo-relationships with people of all ages without the benefit of parental wisdom and protection. How can a parent maintain sovereignty over a child's use of a technology that seems completely foreign?

8. Parental Guilt

Let's face it: some parents know early on that they are ill-suited or ill-prepared for parenthood. Some are quite immature themselves. Many of these parents are more committed to befriending their children and avoiding what they perceive as hypocrisy than they are to holding their children to high standards of behavior. As a result, many parents are unwilling to expect their children to maintain safety when they themselves engage in unsafe behaviors. They feel they would be hypocritical to demand respectful speech and behavior if they refuse to act respectfully toward authorities. They cannot require obedience when they willingly break laws and even scoff at them. Finally, they can hardly expect their children to work hard when they hardly value work enough to maintain their own job.

9. Making Up for Extreme Parenting

If you grew up in a household with authoritarian parents (the "Captain von Trapp Parenting Method"), you know how intolerable that can be. Children who grew up with parents who were too controlling and who stifled their creativity, joy, and playfulness often reject that template of parenting and become committed to erring on the opposite end of the spectrum. It is as if the parent says, "I'm not going to control my children because I remember what that did to me and my siblings!" In swinging the pendulum hard to the opposite side, they begin to parent with the belief that being in control of one's children is a bad thing.

10. Philosophical Differences

Some parents genuinely believe that families should be mini-democracies, where every person's opinion carries equal weight and all persons have equal freedom. One example of what I call a child-first (as opposed to a parent-first or marriage-first) philosophy or wimpy parenting is Aware Parenting, based on the works of Dr. Aletha Solter. This philosophy espouses several sensible principles, including encouraging parents to "spend time each day giving full attention to their children. During this special, quality time, they observe, listen, respond, and join in their children's play (if invited to do so), but they do not direct the children's activities." (*Tears and Tantrums*)

So far, so good. But in the same book, she also describes good parents as realizing "that they cannot prevent all sadness, anger, or frustration, and they do not attempt to stop children from releasing painful feelings through crying or raging." Sorry, but when your eight-year-old begins cussing at you for making him pause his video game so that he can come to dinner, you not only have the right but the responsibility to stop him. You do not entertain such nonsense. While he has every right to feel frustrated, you do not legitimize his expression by allowing it to disrupt the rest of your family's evening. You do not stop loving him at that moment, but you do not express affection for him at that moment either. The real world does not work that way; neither should parents.

As you can see, there are many reasons why some parents have not embraced the idea of a parent-led hierarchy or have not been able to establish themselves as in charge. I hope I have convinced you that it is in the best interest of your child, yourself, and your relationships to establish a proper family hierarchy, with you in charge. It's time you become a Parent in Charge.

Chapter 2
Playing Your Wii Is <u>Not</u> in the Bill of Rights

Those who have lived in a house with spoiled children must have a lively recollection of the degree of torment they can inflict upon all who are within sight or hearing.

~Maria Edgeworth

He had discovered a great law of human action, without knowing it—namely, that in order to make a man or a boy covet a thing, it is only necessary to make the thing difficult to obtain.

~Mark Twain, *The Adventures of Tom Sawyer*

31

Cindy

"My daughter just won't listen. I tell her to keep her cell phone off at night, because I hear her at midnight talking to God knows who. And I have no idea how late she is up talking; I know it is past 11:30. And then she's a pill in the morning and she barks at me and I can't get her to do anything I say."

"Well, Cindy, what do you think of what your mom said?"

Silence. An almost imperceptible shrug of the shoulders. Eyes locked on an iPod.

Wimpy parents frequently find their children developing into teenagers like Cindy, a thirteen-year-old child who was functioning quite well outside of the home. She earned good grades, had positive reports from her teachers and other parents, and even excelled at two sports. Inside the home was a different story altogether. This respected and successful teen exhibited all the major symptoms of GAS: Gnarly Adolescent Syndrome. She was sullen, distant, and disobedient. If attitude were natural gas, they could have heated their home all winter for free.

Cindy's mom had bought into the myth that adolescents were supposed to be sullen, distant, and disobedient. But do not be deceived. There is nothing acceptable or normal about blatant sullenness, disobedience, or disrespect, at any stage of development. Adolescence is *not* a disease, no matter what the popular cultural jokes might suggest.

"So Mom, who pays for Cindy's cell phone?"

Sheepish look. "I do."

"So you're basically paying her to disrespect and disobey you ..."

"What? No, I punish her. It just doesn't do anything—at least, not enough to make her stop."

"I notice that she is playing with an iPod. I'm guessing that this is pretty important to her."

"Yes, she's either on that, the computer, or her cell phone constantly. That's all she does."

"So when she misuses her cell phone, you take that away. But then she is on the computer, chatting with friends, or isolating with her iPod?"

"Yes."

"So, essentially, she knows that if you take away one highly rewarding privilege, she will just focus her attention on another. It's like taking a dollar away from her, but you're giving her four quarters in return. She does not need any of those—her cell phone, computer, or iPod. Those are privileges, not rights."

Cindy shot me an angry and disbelieving glance. Was I really suggesting that her mother should take away her iPod, cell phone, and computer? She had a right to these, didn't she?

Rights versus Privileges

Many parents struggle to discipline their children because they fail to differentiate between rights and privileges. Parents generally want to give their children a fun, enriching lifestyle, so they allow many enjoyable toys, gadgets, and freedoms. This is fine, but children do not naturally understand the difference between those things that are rights and those that are privileges. It is critical that parents understand the difference, teach their children, and accurately apply them both.

Rights are those things automatically granted by an authority; they are not earned. The *Declaration of Independence* lists rights "endowed by their Creator," while the *United States Constitution* includes a Bill of Rights that enumerates many of its citizens' individual rights. These rights are owed to all citizens, whether those citizens work for them or not. For example, our country presumes the right to a fair trail for all citizens, regardless of how heinous the accused crime and how despicable the criminal might be.

On the other hand, *privileges* are those rewards an authority gives only when they are earned. For example, driving a car is not a right; one cannot simply go demand a driver's license. Potential drivers must earn their license by first taking a class, passing written and driving tests, completing a certain number of practice hours, and paying a fee. Those who do not meet these criteria do not receive a license.

Wimpy parents tend to confuse rights and privileges. They allow their children to possess and use video games, use the family computer (or their own computer), watch TV, spend time with their friends, have sleepovers, eat snacks and desserts, and have many other rewards without insisting they be earned. One set of parents I worked with allowed their fifteen-year-old son full use of the family computer, hours of freedom playing video games, and a cell phone (they even *paid for it!),* despite the fact the boy was failing two classes and doing zero chores around the house. They were somehow surprised to discover a complete absence of motivation to do chores or his homework. Helloooo!!!??? With all the rewards he was getting for free, why in the world *would* he work for anything?

I love my work. It is incredibly rewarding to witness the emotional fruits of my labor. However, the primary reason I work hard is for money. My need to take care of my family highly motivates me to do good work, in order to get paid well enough to support my family. Now imagine if I rarely showed up for work, and on the rare occasion I did, I did nothing but e-mail my friends, trade stocks, cut my fingernails, and play Sudoku. Sounds kinda nice, doesn't it?

If you were my client, would you pay me? Of course not; you would be a lunatic to pay me for work I did not do. You would recognize that I had broken our contract—that unwritten agreement whereby I promise to work hard to help you with whatever problem you bring me and you agree to pay me in return.

Now, let's say for a moment that you temporarily lost your mind and decided to pay me anyway. Would you predict that I would work harder as a result, or would I be content to sit at home and play with my kids, watch movies, and hang out at the coffee house? You get the point.

Unemployment Benefits for Children

Similarly, when parents make the mistake of offering privileges without insisting that they are first earned, children begin to develop a sense of entitlement about privileges and, more importantly, their position in the family. Children who receive privileges regardless of their behavior begin to presume that those privileges are actually theirs by right. They are encouraged to believe they are entitled to be served. Worse yet, they make no connection between their behavior and the privileges; this makes them feel powerless.

Many parents come to me and say that they have tried taking privileges away from their children, but are surprised when the response has been hysteria or outright mutiny. Upon close reflection, however, it becomes clear that they never took away any privileges at all, because those things were never earned in the first place. Because they had always been given regardless of behavior, they were perceived as rights. And what do normal people do when they feel their rights have been violated or taken from them? They rebel!

If you are anything like me, you want your children to develop a solid work ethic. You want them to believe that hard work pays off—that good things come to those who work for their rewards. Parents in Charge begin this lesson early on. Unless you are wealthy enough to have full-time maid or cleaning service, there should be no shortage of work available in your home for your child to perform. If this is the case, put your child to volunteer work with neighbors or charitable organizations. Rewarding them with privileges they have not worked for becomes a form of child welfare. Make them earn their rewards now, and you will guarantee them a template for future industriousness.

Chapter Three will explain the Four Expectations that children must meet in order to earn privileges, so there should be no way your child has nothing to do to earn them. Put your kids to work!

Children's Rights

Of course, children also have basic rights. You should afford some things to your children regardless of what they do, how they behave, and what your relationship is like with them. Yes, even your teenager with Gnarly Adolescent Syndrome. These things need not be earned. It is important that your children know that no matter what, you will not renege on your responsibility to take care of them. Here are some basic rights that parents should give their children:

1. Love

This one is somewhat obvious, but let me clarify. I don't mean the warm fuzzy feeling you get when you cuddle your newborn or gaze at your snoozing cherub. I have sat with plenty of parents who genuinely struggle with the temptation to throw their child against the wall or sell their adolescent into slavery. I can't blame some of them; I've met their children.

Parenting normal children means parenting children who are sometimes difficult, obnoxious, selfish, and ridiculous. Bill Cosby called them "brain-damaged." I call them "normal kids." All normal parents loathe their children from time to time. I've been there. I have the permanent-marker "artwork" all over my bedroom furniture to remind me.

Good and bad feelings come and go. But love isn't about feelings. It's about making French toast for your daughter after she wakes you up (in spite of telling her for the fourteenth time not to wake you before 6:00 AM on your only day off). It's about eagerly forgiving your son the moment he shows remorse for spilling the last of the milk, even though now he can't have cereal and the cupboards are pretty thin. It's about listening to that inane, meandering, so-boring-you-want-to-puke story when you know she just wants to drag out bedtime and you just want to go to bed.

That's the stuff you do for your children no matter how gnarly, how obnoxious, or how ridiculous they have recently been.

2. Valid, fair discipline

All Americans have the right to a fair trial. Your children should also have the right to a fair trial in your home when it comes to matters of discipline. They have the right to parents who claim the mantle of authority, who are in control of themselves, and who mete out justice fairly.

They have the right to be heard when rules are made or changed or when they believe they have been wronged. This doesn't mean you will agree with them or acquiesce to them, but listening to them is key. Sometimes, you will be wrong in your judgments; freely admitting a mistake does your child and your relationship a world of good.

3. Knowledge of rules and expectations

Children should not be kept in the dark about the rules and expectations of the home. They need boundaries and the predictability that comes from knowing what is expected of them. The rules and expectations should be clear. Chapter Three will help you make your expectations crystal clear.

4. Freedom of religion

Each child has a conscience. He deserves to have it respected by allowing him the right to believe what he chooses about God and other worldview matters. Parents own the awesome responsibility to teach their children about God, ethics, and worldviews. But they also have a duty to allow them to draw their own conclusions about these matters.

You may expect behaviors that are consistent with your worldview. For example, you can expect your children to attend church or synagogue with you. If they refuse to go because of professed differences of belief, it is important to not argue with them. Simply tell them that you respect their right to believe differently, that they need not believe what you do, but it is very important to spend family time together and learn how to be with people who disagree with one's worldview or religion. Someday, your child will attend a wedding or funeral in a church or a bar/bat mitzvah at a synagogue.

Remember, you will never succeed if you try to control your child's thoughts. Try to control what swims around in their minds and I guarantee you will incite rebellion. Good luck with that.

5. Freedom of (respectful) speech

Your children do not have the right to yell or scream at you when they are upset (unless they are bleeding out of their ears or the house is on fire). They do not have the right to call you "retarded" or "stupid," or respond to a question with "Whatever." They do not have the right to defy you, verbally or silently.

However, they do have the right to disagree with you and even debate you *if they are able to do so with respect*. Parents in Charge recognize that teaching children how to engage in lively, respectful disagreement and debate constitutes an important part of a child's development. Allow your child to disagree with phrases like, "I respectfully disagree" or "I don't see it that way; let me tell you why."

6. Food, clothing, shelter

As much as you might be tempted, you cannot kick your child out of the house without food, clothing, and a place to stay—at least not until he or she is eighteen. Until then, it is your job to provide your child with life's necessities. On the other hand, this does not mean that your child has the right to the most fashionable and expensive clothes on the market. When your child reaches working age, his expensive clothing, fast food, and snacks should be covered by money he earns at home or money he earns from a part-time job.

Also, your child does not have the right to every meal or dessert at every meal. If your children are rude at the dinner table or do not eat a healthy meal, you would be nuts to reward them with dessert. Sending Junior to bed without dinner can be a quick and effective way to curb some of his nastier behaviors (although this method should be used sparingly). He's not going to starve to death from missing one dinner.

7. Freedom of thought

Just as children have the right to believe what they want about God and other worldview matters, they have the right to think whatever they want about anything. Not only is it impossible to control the thoughts of children, it is not desirable.[3]

8. Freedom to feel

Another thing you simply cannot control: feelings. If your child wants to feel angry at you, that is her prerogative. If your child's feelings seem ridiculous to you, that's because you don't understand him enough. This does not mean that your child may *express* his feelings in any way or at any time he desires. If I'm angry, I don't have the right to punch a hole in the wall. If your child is angry, she has the right to express herself, but only in ways that are safe and respectful.

9. Be informed about medical treatments

I am alarmed by the number of children who are prescribed psychiatric medications to make them more successful or obedient, or to curb symptoms of depression or anxiety. With all due respect, I think it is fundamentally the wrong choice. At the same time, I empathize with the difficulty parents face when their child struggles emotionally or behaviorally. I respect their right to treat their child in the way they deem best.[4]

What I cannot respect and find deplorable is withholding information from children about the real risks of psychiatric medications

---

3   Unless your child likes bad music; then it is your *duty* to control their thinking.
4   Many of my child patients are on psychiatric medication. If the parents are comfortable with it, then I withhold any and all judgment.

and other treatments. I have encountered innumerable school-age children taking stimulants who have no idea why they aren't hungry for lunch, why they are depressed or zombie-like during the day, why they can't sleep at night, why they get "goofy" in the late afternoon, why they are obsessively lining up pencils and other things, and why they have developed strange tics. There are also the millions of children and teenagers taking "antidepressants" like Zoloft and Lexapro, who are never told about the risks of mania, akathisia (which directly causes suicidal thoughts and impulses), and the high probability of sexual dysfunction.

Children have a right to know the truth about the drugs we are putting into their brain and the real risks of other medical treatments. If they cannot handle the truth, they should probably be free from that kind of chemical or medical intrusion.

10. Some privacy

Privacy is a bit tricky; it is both a right and a privilege. Developmentally, your child needs some privacy in order to explore himself and the world. She needs to have private conversations, talk about you behind your back, and try out her funky new dance moves behind closed doors. One sure-fire way to destroy your relationship with your child is to deny him or her an appropriate modicum of privacy.

On the other hand, Parents in Charge dole out privacy only to the degree that safety allows. For example, if your teenager has a history of talking to strangers online, she should not be granted the privacy of going online. You would be crazy to allow her to go online by herself in the interest of respecting her privacy.[5] Similarly, if your four-year-old can't wipe himself properly, you're going to have to check to make sure he doesn't leave the house a walking stench.

11. Sexual integrity

This one shouldn't have to be said, but because a child's innocence is one of his or her most precious and fragile qualities, it must be emphasized. Children have the right not to be sexualized. Their bodies

---

5   It is no coincidence that the words "privacy" and "privilege" stem from the same root word.

are theirs. They have a right not to be subjected to or privy to sexually charged material, such as pornography and sexually provocative talk. They have a right to explore their own bodies (in private) without judgment.

12. Not be physically misused/abused

Duhhh. I'm going to cover corporal punishment in Chapter 10, so there will remain no doubt what constitutes physical abuse and what doesn't.

13. Not be emotionally abused, bullied

This one is not as simple as one might think. Obviously, parents who call their children cruel names or try to squash their sense of self-worth are evil and should be put in the gulag. But what about more innocent teasing and name-calling? When my daughter leaves the house for school without her backpack, is it cruel to say, "Hey Blondie, you forgot your backpack again?" Well, it all depends.

Some parents know how to say things like this with a glimmer in their eye. There is a clear message that says, "I love you; you are silly. Get your backpack." One of the ways we love each other in my home is by calling each other "dork." In some homes that would be highly inappropriate. In ours, "dork" is a term of endearment. Of course, I'm the Chief Dork, so I don't escape the teasing. No one in our home feels emotionally abused or bullied when called a benign name.

Essentially, anything that purposely or inadvertently makes your children feel less loved, valuable, or worthwhile should be stricken from your vocabulary.

Rights versus Privileges

The following table shows a list of rights and privileges. Study the lists. Are you treating some privileges as rights? Are you going to the other extreme and forcing your child to earn something that should be hers as a right? Talk with your spouse or support person to help clarify which might need to be changed in your home.

Rights versus Privileges

	Rights	Privileges
Definition:	Things you may have or do simply because you are a human and are part of this family	Things you are allowed to do that must be earned by being safe, respectful, obedient, and doing your work
Result when not given:	Rebellion Righteous anger	Disappointment Often working harder to earn
Examples:	Love Valid, fair discipline Knowledge of rules, expectations Freedom of religion Freedom of speech (respectful) Food, clothing, shelter Freedom of thought Freedom to feel Treated with fairness Be informed about medical treatments Some privacy Sexual integrity Not be physically misused/abused Not be emotionally abused, bullied	Driver's license, use of the car iPod Video Games T.V. Computer/Internet Cell Phone (and use of it) Sleepovers Having friends over Choice of music Concerts Going out Dating Attention Money Use of own money Speaking to parents like adults Choosing schedule (e.g., when homework and chores are done)
What happens when granted in spite of misbehavior	Feel respected, cared for Sometimes gratefulness results in behavior/attitude change	Sense of entitlement Child confuses privilege with right Unmotivated to respect or obey Confusion/indignation when parent makes demands

Chapter 3

Nothing More, Nothing Less: The Four Expectations Parents Can and Should Have For Their Children

Always obey your parents, when they are present.

~Mark Twain

Don't handicap your children by making their lives easy.

~Robert A. Heinlein

Great Expectations

Parents have a million dreams for their children. They all desire them to be intelligent, beautiful, compassionate, talented (hopefully enough for a full college scholarship), helpful, happy, and tolerant. Sure, parents say that they just want a healthy child with ten toes and ten fingers, but most parents would have to admit they want their child to have more and be more, both for the child's benefit and, let's face it, for theirs.

But what can we really expect from our children? Is it fair to expect them to be highly intelligent? Are we failing our children if they don't have talent enough to qualify for the Olympics or make the final round of the National Spelling Bee? Is it enough that they are happy?

Let me be clear: *it is not your job as a parent to secure your child's happiness*. Making that your primary goal would be a colossal mistake. First, children need to figure this out on their own; they cannot be reliant on others for regulating their happiness. Second, trying to make another person happy is a task far too consuming for any mortal. Like Sisyphus rolling the great boulder up a mountain only to see it speed right back down, it is impossible to grant your children an abiding, deep happiness. I do not mean that parental love and sacrifice contribute little to children's happiness; they certainly are integral to building a child's sense of happiness and joy. But they are simply insufficient. Children need their parents to not only love them but to establish and maintain limits, to train them in myriad of ways, and to make the frequent choice to place the child's needs ahead of his wants.

For example, when my son was three, he would frequently ask for a cookie or another dessert after dinner. My wife or I would often allow him one, provided he has eaten enough healthy food during dinner and he asks politely (yes, three-year-olds should be expected to ask politely for things and should never be given something if they are rude, demanding, or whiny. Start the process early and future limit setting will be easier; wait until they are older and it will be infinitely more difficult). If he asked for another cookie after his first and his mother and I determined that one was enough, we were left with a difficult choice. We knew that he would feel upset not getting the cookie and would likely show us his displeasure in a typical three-year-old manner: crying, begging, and demanding.

45

Parents who give in to requests like these will indeed result in pleasure. One might even say that parents can induce a temporary, superficial happiness. But this is not the kind of happiness children need. More importantly, we are not responsible for providing children pleasure. Our commission as parents involves teaching self-control, demonstrating the reality that life is full of limits and frustrations, and teaching them that certain things are special and are enjoyed best in moderation. In those teachable moments, parents will offer their child one or the other: short-term pleasure or a long-term life lesson.

Our training should prepare our children for future careers, enable them to navigate future relationships, and encourage good citizenship. In order to train them, the expectations need to be established early on and maintained throughout childhood. Our expectations for our children should be neither too great nor too small. Essentially, there are four overarching expectations that parents should have for their children. When they meet these expectations, they will be on their way toward a solid career, excellent relationships, and model citizenship, with the bonus that we desire for them: a deep, abiding happiness.

The Four Expectations

1. *Safety*

The foundation of our responsibility to our children and the precursor to all other expectations is safety. If your child cannot maintain his or others' safety, then it won't matter if he gets his homework done, follows curfew, or practices his piano lessons. Safety here refers to how well your child maintains his own safety and that of his family members, your home, and your possessions.

First, your child must know that he may not under any circumstances use illicit drugs or alcohol. Prescription drugs must only be used under strict supervision and within parental limits. There should be no negotiating this issue.

Note: This includes cigarettes. Now, some parents go easy on their teens with smoking, but answer this: would you allow your child to drink poison a few times a day, every day? I presume not. If you love your child that much, why in the world would you allow him to smoke cigarettes? If the answer has anything to do with allowing him freedom, the significant addictive nature of nicotine, the widespread use of cigarettes, or the relative innocence of cigarettes compared to harder drugs, then I challenge you to reconsider.

Cigarettes are not only illegal for children and against the rules at almost every middle school and high school, but they are likely to cause grave danger to your child and cost your family money. Also, the nicotine in cigarettes is a highly addictive stimulant. Please know that addiction to one stimulant often predicts future addiction to another stimulant. This is not something you want to support. In essence, allowing that kind of nonsense is, well, nonsensical.

Alcohol use is a touchy subject for many families who believe that occasional, parent-monitored alcohol use is acceptable. Granted, some researchers suggest that making all alcohol taboo fosters the "If it's naughty, I wanna do it" mentality that can get adolescents or even young children in trouble. Others are committed to the idea that allowing children small amounts of alcohol will demystify it and encourage more sensible attitudes and habits in the future. It is also important to note that many cultures more readily accept childhood or adolescent use of alcohol (in small amounts) for family gatherings, religious ceremonies, and the like. Obviously, allowing your child to get drunk at a party is insane, as it is extremely dangerous, both physically and legally.

My wife and I decided that our children should be allowed a sip of our wine or beer (not cocktails) at dinner or during a party. Not a glass or several sips; just a sip. We have discovered a few important phenomena as a result of this decision. First, we now know who has a natural taste for alcohol (i.e., my son; my daughters both respond to alcohol as if they are imbibing a mixture of sewage and razor blades). Second, we take notice of each child's attitude toward alcohol. For example, my eldest knew she was doing something adult and a bit out of the ordinary, so we knew we needed to discuss the realities of alcohol a bit more carefully with her. Third, we saw how each child was extremely interested in our use of alcohol and were curious what it means that we choose to consume alcohol. This has given us several opportunities to discuss alcohol openly, especially as it pertains to self-control and the family expectations regarding alcohol. Finally, this choice has forced my wife and me to focus on how we model self-control and prudence with our alcohol use.

In the end, either decision is valid, provided you are committed to modeling appropriate behavior and attitudes.

Your child must not hurt herself purposely in any way, including cutting, burning, scarring (a form of tattooing not involving ink, but burn or cut marks), starving or restricting food, or high-risk behaviors such as drag-racing, roof-jumping, pyromania, or having "Amateur World Wrestling" night in your backyard. Regarding the latter, I am not referring to some activities that can legitimately be considered high-risk but are not likely to cause grave injury. For example, enjoying roller coasters, whitewater rafting, scuba diving, Karate (formal training, not "Amateur Karate Kid Night" with the buddies), innocent campfire activity, sibling/friend wrestling, playground showing off, and skating tricks are all normal, healthy activities that can help children negotiate risk-taking but are not necessarily unsafe. Here is a good rule of thumb: if you would be embarrassed to have your child's activity shown on YouTube, you probably shouldn't let your children do it.

Regarding healthy eating behavior, this is where it is important to walk the fine line between being *in control* of your child and controlling your child. Food intake—quantity and quality—is something that parents can generally control when children are younger. Now, I am not at all suggesting that parents control the amount an infant consumes; most infants have no trouble self-regulating their food intake. Whether they are bottle- or breast-fed, babies know when they have had enough and when they are still hungry.

Toddlers too tend to be naturally self-regulating when it comes to the quantity of food they consume. The major exception is the phenomenon of vegetables suppressing the appetite, which magically reawakens two minutes later with the presence of dessert. By and large, toddlers and young children are not independent enough to make wise decisions about what kinds of food they should eat. Parents not only have a right but a responsibility to be in control of their child's food choices.

However, the developmental task of regulating food intake is one that should slowly be given to the child as soon as he or she shows the ability to make responsible choices. Parents who allow too little freedom by enforcing too many food rules are likely to find their children fighting them in subtle ways. As many professionals can testify, this begins a dangerous cycle of conflict surrounding food and control.

On the other hand, until the child is an adolescent, parents can be too willy-nilly about their child's diet. Children should not be allowed to eat whatever they want, whenever they want. Dieticians have sounded the alarm that parents err greatly when they allow children to eat fast food, soda, Starbucks, and sweets whenever they like. Some simple, reasonable rules not only make sense, but help children develop healthy eating patterns. Of course, this represents one of those areas where modeling healthy choices is essential.

A note about caffeine: caffeine is a potent central nervous system stimulant. As such, it has a potential for addiction—almost as much as cocaine. In small doses, it is relatively harmless; it can temporarily improve mood, energy level, attention and focus, and can mask sleep deficiency during the daytime. However, parents need to know that any central nervous stimulant can cause obsessive-compulsive patterns, increase anxiety, cause agitation, cause or worsen insomnia, and even bring on intense, rageful fantasies. For children, whose nervous systems are relatively immature, regular caffeine use is not a good idea. So forget the Starbucks runs, unless you can make certain that your child gets something without caffeine.

Once your child enters the promised land of adolescence, your ability to control their diet diminishes. Your teen will frequently eat out at friends' houses and other public places. As this happens, it is crucial that you recognize and communicate your inability to control your child. Acknowledging this, while communicating a caring attitude, is the best you can do, as long as the child's diet does not become unsafe.

Sexual activity is also subsumed under this category. I don't care what your child is learning in school: sexual activity before marriage is dangerous, both physically and emotionally. Obviously, intercourse is far riskier than making out or even petting; similarly, sex without a condom is far more "unprotected" than sex with one. But any sexual activity (other than masturbation) should be considered unsafe and against the family rules.

So what rules can or should parents make about sexual activity? The answer to that depends on your beliefs regarding sexual norms and what limits you would like for your children. My advice: don't be shy. Don't put your child's sexual activity into the "It's her body; we don't have the right to legislate what she does with it" category too soon. While it is absolutely crucial that you protect your child's sexual integrity by given him or her privacy in sexual matters, this privacy is not absolute.

Remember that one of your responsibilities as the one in charge is to protect your child's emotional and physical safety until she is able to do it for herself. Until your child is well into adolescence, you have the right as parents to decide when your child dates, when he or she is allowed to be alone with the opposite sex, what level of sex education he or she has, how he or she dresses, and how much sexual material (on TV, movies, music, websites) is acceptable.

2. Respect

Respect here refers to treating all persons and possessions according to their value and position. While my daughter and my wife have equal value as human beings, I don't treat them the same. I have a different respect for my wife's position as wife, mother, and adult. Similarly, our children should be taught to approach police officers, teachers, friends' parents, and most adults with a more humble and obedient attitude than that which they approach their friends.

I know others disagree with me on the following point, but I find it ludicrous that children call adults—even neighbors and friends' parents—by their first name. Here, we would be wise to learn something from our southern friends, who tend to teach children to address adults in a formal manner. When we address an adult in front of our children, they pick up on the level of respect that is being paid to that person. If I drop off my daughter to a friend's house for the afternoon, saying "Now remember that Mrs. Dannon is going to give you lunch; you remember your manners, OK?" communicates a subtly different message about Mrs. Dannon than if I simple use her first name. Words are powerful, especially when used to address people.

A person's name still holds a great deal of his or her esteem. Think about it: "Dr. Einstein" engenders more respect than "Al"; "Sergeant Smith" sounds more honorable than "Officer Bill." And "Ms. Michaels" holds a more adult and respectable air than "Jenny" or even "Miss

Jenny." If we expect our children to respect and esteem their elders, then they should be expected to refer to them by the position that has earned them that respect or, at a minimum, by their surname.

Please do not misunderstand me. I am not suggesting a caste-like system where doctors and lawyers are "worth" more respect than farmers or the mailman. Lawyer jokes aside, I don't think any sane person would suggest that a lawyer has more worth (or is therefore worthy of more respect) than a mailman. All respectable adults should be honored with a title of respect. In my practice, I request that children call me "Dr. Paterno" or "Dr. P.", at least at the beginning of our work together. I ask that the parents call me "Dr. Paterno" or "Dr. P." in their child's presence; in private, I don't mind if parents use my first name.

Children should be taught that all family members must respect all other family members, including parents, siblings, grandparents, aunts, uncles, and cousins. They should also be taught that they must respect their and others' property, as well as themselves.

There are several forms of respect. The first is **verbal respect.** One of the most important ways we exhibit respect for others is with our spoken words. Specifically, children must be taught how crucial it is to speak kindly in word and tone both to and about family members.

Some examples of disrespect that some parents learn to tolerate include:

- Rolling eyes when spoken to
- Saying loudly, "I know!"
- Defying (saying "No!" to a command)
- Lying
- Correcting adults in a challenging, unloving way
- Not looking at adults when spoken to
- "Storming" out of the room: huffing and puffing sighs, stomping

None of these should be tolerated, even during the adolescent years. A good rule of thumb is this: if it shouldn't be done to a judge in a courtroom, it shouldn't be allowed in relationship with parents. A judge certainly wouldn't tolerate any of these; neither should parents.

Another benchmark I use with parents is this: think of what your child says or does to you. What would have happened if you said or did that to your parents? Almost every parent I use this with gets a look of horror on their face: "I would have lost my teeth if I talked like that to my father!" or "We wouldn't have even thought of talking like that. We don't even know what would have happened, but we just knew not to cross that line."

So why are we even considering allowing our children to speak to us with disrespectful words, tones, or behaviors? Why are we allowing children to wear t-shirts that boast, flaunt disrespect, or champion stupidity? It's time to stop letting our children get away with this nonsense and time to insist on respectful, well-behaved children!

Physical respect refers to respecting the personal space of others. Children should learn at an early age that each person has a personal "bubble" around him that is a sacred space. No one should intrude on that space unless it is invited and it is safe.

Note: Games like "tag," football, and others that include bodily contact are completely appropriate (and are healthy, fun activities that should be allowed, *especially* during school P.E. and recess periods), as long as the rules of the game are being followed and don't become overly aggressive.

Some examples of physical disrespect are:
- Excessive, unwelcome affection (e.g., bear hugs, kissing)
- Sexually suggestive touching (e.g., goosing, spanking, bra-snapping, "pantsing")
- Uninvited wrestling, boxing, gang-tackling, and other forms of aggressive play

Now, before I hear from every athlete who has patted a teammate on the butt or whipped someone with a towel in the locker room, understand that I am referring to *unwelcome* boundary violations. When I was in high school, our sports teams certainly gave our share of wedgies, swirlies, and noogies. This was a socially acceptable, albeit bizarre, way of expressing camaraderie and affection among teammates. None of us would have supported any of these if done in a cruel way or toward an unsupportive victim. In the sports culture, some forms of aggression are actually expressions of affection and approval.

Children should be taught to **respect property** by maintaining the safety and privacy of others' things and space.

Some examples are:
- Not going in siblings' room without permission (for older children/teens)
- Not touching "special" belongings (e.g., iPod, diary) without permission
- Stealing
- Not defacing or otherwise damaging others' things
- Respecting the cars by not leaving messes

Respect for your body: Taking reasonable care of yourself
- Hygiene: showering regularly, brushing teeth, trimming nails, toileting, using deodorant (for adolescents)
- Not marking the body with tattoos, piercings, telephone numbers

Note: many adolescents put a great deal of pressure on their parents to allow piercings or tattoos; some parents don't have strong feelings about them. Notwithstanding my opinion that this is crazy, the point here is that if it is acceptable to the parents, it must be done with the parents' permission or blessing. It should go without saying that both parents should agree on this limit before anything is allowed.

3. Obedience

Simply put, obedience refers to two qualities: complying with requests and commands and following house rules. Other than respect, this is easily the biggest problem in households today. Children are not obeying their parents and their rules nearly as well as they should, while parents are not insisting on proper obedience.

The first part of the obedience expectation can be simply put: do what you are told, when you are told, without arguing, debating, complaining, or dawdling. By the age of three or four, almost all children should be expected to acknowledge a command, verbally assent to it, and comply with it in short order.

One exception to this expectation: you cannot expect your child to comply with a command when given from another room and when your child is in the middle of a video game, television program, or similarly engrossing activity. For many children, these activities require so much concentration that they simply will not hear a command from another room—their brains are not equipped to attend to distant auditory information. If you want your engrossed child to comply with a command, you will have to interrupt his or her field of vision (which means you'll have to be in the same room), make certain you have his full attention, and then give the command. Or, better yet, don't let Junior play video games or watch TV!

Some parents might take exception to the word "command." For some, it sounds too militaristic, Old Testament, or severe. I have asked parents for a better word than command; some prefer "direction" or "instruction." I can see teachers preferring the latter, but following directions sounds more like completing a recipe than showing submission to an authority. However, if those phrases are preferable to you, use them. The point is the same: you are the boss and you expect your child to do what he is told.

One mistake I see parents making is <u>The Recommendation</u>: "Hey Jonah, I think you should go get your backpack; the bus is just about here." Well, isn't that nice of her to share her thoughts on the matter? The problem is that your child can just as easily reply, "Thanks for the recommendation, Mom; I think I'm going to sit here and play *Mario Brothers* for a few more minutes."

Another similar mistake is <u>The Quiz</u>: "Jonah, do you know what's coming soon? What do you think you should do right now?" Your child might get the hint, but it's not exactly obedience inspiring. Your hinting will do little but annoy your child, and, when he does not respond as you desire, you will soon become annoyed.

Yet another mistake is <u>The Request</u>: "Hey Jonah, why don't you go get your backpack?" This one welcomes sarcasm and all kinds of humorous responses, such as, "Because I don't feel like it" or "Why don't <u>you</u> go get it for me?"

Forget those. Wimpy assistant managers use those. You are not an assistant manager of your home. You are the parent—the sovereign of your family. Because you love your children, you do not make requests or suggestions when it comes to their safety, health, and well-being. You give commands, orders, mandates, and you expect them to obey you. Issue your commands confidently and in order form: "Get your backpack; the bus is almost here."

You'll notice that this order is coupled with a reason. Essentially, you want the child to obey a particular order for a particular reason. We should not expect constant blind obedience from our children; it is entirely understandable that they wish to know why you are commanding them. Sometimes you have the time and patience to explain your commands to them. When you do, explain yourself. You may find that your commands are silly, unnecessary, or motivated by selfishness or laziness. In that case, edit or cancel your command.

If you don't have time or you don't wish to get into a significant dialogue about why your daughter should pick up her room the night before the cleaning lady comes, then you rely on your backup explanation: "Trust me; there is a good reason" or "Because I will make your life miserable if you don't." Your word and command should be enough. Your child may sometimes need to obey blindly; here you have your history of trustworthiness and ability to follow through on consequences to rely on.

4. *Work*

Work here refers to two major responsibilities: schoolwork and chores. Children should be required to perform to the best of their abilities in school. For most children, this means that their child must:

- attend school every day unless they are bleeding profusely or are on fire, in which case, they can stay home until a band-aid has been applied or the fire department is done dousing them. School refusal is simply not an option (I will discuss school refusal in greater detail in Chapter 10).
- complete 100% of assigned homework and hand it in *on time.*
- achieve test and quiz grades up to his or her potential (for most children, this means C's and above).
- behave appropriately during the school day, including bus rides and unstructured times (recess, after-school activities).

Chores refers to both daily and weekly chores. From the age of four or so, children should be given daily and weekly chores. This extremely important developmental task fosters a sense of communal responsibility, an appreciation of work, and a special appreciation of the amount of work that parents perform for the family.

Chores must be completed on time. A set time for chore completion makes sense, although exceptions due to after-school activities should be accommodated. Chores should also be completed satisfactorily, according to parents' standards. If the parents decide that the bed should be made with two pillows on it, then the bed is not made satisfactorily if only one pillow is on it. Raise your expectations of your children and you will raise their expectations of themselves.

My younger daughter has a list of chores that includes two daily chores that take about five minutes, as well as two weekly chores that she must perform on Saturday. Both daily and weekly chores must be completed before she may have any free time or may go to any of her activities. One day she asked us, "Where is your chore list?" My wife and I were able to rattle off a partial list of our daily "chores." When we had listed about 40 items, she stopped us and said, "I only have to do two? I'm glad I'm not a grown-up." Later on that night, as my wife was cooking dinner and I was emptying the dishwasher, she added, "Mom, you do a lot of work that I don't have to do. Now I know why you like to rest after we go to bed." That provided one of those "Ahhh, life is good" moments.

One final note on chores: when your child turns eight or so, she can be expected to remember to do her chore immediately when she gets home from school. You simply must make a chart with the list of daily chores in her room or in the kitchen. Something like this works well:

Monday	Tuesday	Wednesday	Thursday	Friday	Weekend
Put all shoes and jackets away	Wipe all screens with Windex	Put all bikes and other outside toys in garage	Sweep, mop kitchen floor	All books back on shelves	Write letter to Grandma
Garbage out	Dishes	Vacuum room	Cook dinner		Clear cars of garbage, junk

Chapter 4

The Three Exceptions: Disease, Disorder, and Disability

In the final analysis it is not what you do for your children but what you have taught them to do for themselves that will make them successful human beings

~Ann Landers

At every step the child should be allowed to meet the real experiences of life; the thorns should never be plucked from his roses

~Ellen Key, *The Century of the Child*

What About Exceptions?

As with many rules and expectations, there should be some room for exceptions. It would be unrealistic to assume there are no children who would have genuine difficulty meeting the Four Expectations, so let us consider some exceptions to the general rule. This section will be a short one, because the vast majority of children are fully capable of meeting the Four Expectations. The exceptions are few.

Parents must be careful to avoid one of two errors with their children. The first error involves presuming that an able child is unable. Expecting less from someone who can indeed meet an expectation does the child great harm, essentially teaching the child not to strive. Parents must avoid this error, inadvertently or purposely.

An equally dangerous error involves presuming an unable child is able. Imagine demanding that your child with a broken leg run laps in P.E. or insisting that your flu-ridden child complete her homework. Not only would this style of parenting lack compassion, but it would likely bring the local Child Protective Services to your doorstep. Not a good idea.

Essentially, only three factors should alter your expectations for your children. They all conveniently start with D, so they are called the *Three D's*: *Disease, Disorder*, and *Disability*. I will describe each of these, challenge the validity of some common labels often used to lower expectations, and suggest how Parents in Charge can accommodate those children who truly need accommodation.

Disease

It doesn't take an über-parent to recognize that if Junior has a *disease* or illness, you must accommodate him or lower your expectations until the child fully heals. For example, it would be cruel to expect a child with mono to go to school; nor should a child with the swine flu baby-sit her siblings. The child with severe food allergies should not force himself to eat what Grandma makes for dinner if it includes ingredients that will make him sick. All of these should be obvious; I doubt there are few parents who would disagree.

But what do you do if your child has a common viral disease like a cold? Certainly, a cold can make any child miserable and children with colds require more rest than usual. However, should a parent whose child has a cold excuse her from regular responsibilities? Simply stated, no. A child with a cold should continue to perform his or her chores and complete schoolwork on time; of course, there is no reason why that child shouldn't continue to offer respect and maintain safety. Unless the child's pediatrician insists that the need for rest supersedes school attendance, the expectation of going to school should remain. Your child can live with the sniffles or a minor cough.

If Junior does stay home from school because of illness, he should restart homework and chores as soon as possible. While the threshold might be somewhat difficult to determine, here is one guideline that can help: "If you are well enough to focus on TV or video games or you can play outside, you are well enough to catch up on schoolwork." Usually that will induce enough motivation for Junior to get moving.

Disorder

Now, the most nebulous of the Three D's: *disorder*. What exactly is a disorder? Is ADHD a disorder? What about insomnia? Sleep apnea? Test anxiety? Which disorders should induce parents to accommodate and/or lessen their expectations?

Webster's New International Dictionary defines a disorder as *a derangement of function, an abnormal physical or mental condition*. Not very specific. In fact, we all experience abnormal physical and mental conditions. For example, when I watch football games, I tend to become quite excited. My combination of screams, cheers, groans, and dances probably make me appear nothing short of deranged. I suppose this could be considered an abnormal mental condition; but does it constitute a disorder?

Simply stated, the threshold for what we consider abnormal hovers too low. It seems as though almost anything out of the ordinary can be considered a disorder these days. Think about it; if some official sounding team of physicians got together, they could make anything a disorder:

- Obnoxious Disorder
- Religious Fanaticism Disorder
- Pervasive Fastidiousness Disorder
- Extreme Political Views Disorder
- Racism Disorder

Did you know that there is a disorder in the *Diagnostic and Statistical Manual of Mental Disorders* (DSM-IV) called *Intermittent Explosive Disorder*? Essentially, this supposed mental disorder refers to a child who often gets angry...really, really angry. Are you kidding me? It should embarrass the American Psychiatric Association that their bible includes such laughable nonsense. Because almost anything could be considered a disorder, the term's meaning diminishes to meaninglessness.

Another problem is that many people confuse disorder with a medical problem. Problems and struggles that have a label like "disorder" often are presumed to have some medical cause. Given that the psychiatric disorders are defined by physicians, this is no surprise.

So what is a true disorder?

Think about Attention-Deficit/Hyperactivity Disorder (ADHD), the most commonly diagnosed childhood disorder. Mainstream mental health professionals like to refer to ADHD as a neurobiological disorder or a neurobehavioral disorder. Baloney! Are there children who are distracted, lack focus, or to struggle to pay attention in a classroom? Of course. Is it abnormal? Not at all. Especially given the fact that the development of the part of the brain implicated in ADHD—the frontal lobes—often lags behind the rest of the brain, we should expect that a fair number of children will function differently than their peers in their so-called "executive functions." We shouldn't expect all children to function at the same level any more than we should expect all children to be equally intelligent.

At the same time, should we lower our expectations of those children? No! They must be trained to improve those skills. Diagnosing them with some pseudoscientific disorder communicates the wrong message to the child: "You cannot function as well as others because your brain is broken." It also communicates a horrendous message to the parents: "You cannot effect positive change in your child's behavior; he is slave to his broken brain." Wrong. Parents in Charge recognize that they have an enormous impact in their child's life, even in their executive functioning skills.

Rather than lowering your expectations for the child with ADHD-like problems (and believe me, I know there are many children who have them), raise your expectations. Take control of your child's behavior; train him or her.[6] You can "cure" your child of ADHD if you are sufficiently committed, coordinated, and consistent.

Another good example of a pseudo-scientific disorder is *test anxiety*. Now, before I get a slew of hate mail about the reality of test anxiety, let me clarify. I know that many people experience anxiety before and during tests. I recognize that for some, test anxiety does not refer to minor butterflies—some people get extremely uncomfortable pains, upset stomach, sweats, shortness of breath, panicky thoughts, and even tics. I know that the subjective experience can be quite distressful; I know this because I struggled with test anxiety throughout most of my education.

My point is that test anxiety, while uncomfortable and even dysfunctional, is entirely normal and fixable. Almost all anxiety represents a normal physical and emotional response to a set of beliefs and perceptions. In the case of test anxiety, the distress comes from a set of exaggerated beliefs and perceptions about the test—usually about the importance of the test and the possible consequences of performing poorly.

Parents—often with the help of a skilled clinician—can help a child struggling with test anxiety minimize that anxiety, often in a short period. While being empathic and compassionate with the child, the parent should maintain their high expectations for the child. Test anxiety is a real problem, but not a disorder.

Some "disorders" that are valid and warrant serious consideration include:

- *Sleep disorders such as sleep apnea.* If your child is not sleeping, he or she will not function adequately. Luckily, parents and physicians can often fix these problems fairly quickly and decisively.
- *Autism and the Autistic Spectrum Disorders.* Some of these are too liberally diagnosed (such as *Asperger's*), but autism is very likely a true neurological disorder. Some children with autism can function in a normal classroom with accommodations, while others require an alternative academic placement.

---

6   The best book on the market for teaching parents how to train an ADHD-like child is *Unraveling the ADD/ADHD Fiasco* by Dr. David Stein.

- *Elimination Disorders.* Like sleep problems, if your child has difficulty staying dry at night, you can help your child through it fairly quickly and simply. I work with a number of children who struggle with nighttime wetness who are "cured" in a matter of days. Until then, you must accommodate your child, but recognize that he or she should still be held accountable for the Four Expectations.

Disability

Finally, *disability*. Unfortunately, this is another confusing term. Does disabled mean completely unable? Does it presume that the child's limitations are completely out of the child's control and no one can do a thing about it? When I use the term disability, I am referring to any diminished sphere of functioning that the child cannot control, regardless of the child's effort or the effort and skill of the parents to train the child. "Cannot" is the operative word here. If the child can function at a normal level if trained properly, then there is no disability; the child is simply behind in that skill area due to insufficient training or effort.

Take one of the most commonly diagnosed disabilities: Learning Disability. The Learning Disability diagnosis (which includes Dyslexia) is one of the most unscientific labels in existence. In order to reach a diagnosis of LD, the child must show evidence of average or better intelligence, as measured by an IQ test, usually administered by a clinical or school psychologist. Then, the child's overall abilities are contrasted to his or her academic achievement based on a standardized achievement test. If a statistical difference exists, then the psychologist must determine what processing problem is responsible for that difference. Some examples include poor memory, phonological processing (combining sounds and syllables quickly and accurately), sluggish fluency, visual-motor problems, sensory integration weaknesses, and vision problems (such as convergence insufficiency).

Of course there are some children who have weaker functioning in some area of academic functioning. I would never challenge the existence of academic struggles and weaknesses. However, every one of these academic skills is learned and every one of these children is trainable. Every one of them can improve—often dramatically. Compare that with physical disabilities, such as cerebral palsy. Would anyone dare consider that a child with CP can train away the symptoms? No way. The processing problems in learning disabilities are fundamentally different. They can be significantly improved. I have seen it many times.[7] Learning Disabilities represent weaknesses, for sure. But the mainstream literature is wrong; they are not true disabilities.

Danny Boy

Danny remains one of my favorite children of all time. When I first met Danny, he was a diminutive 11-year-old finishing the Fifth Grade. His adoptive parents, Jim and Susan, were a middle-class couple who had adopted him from his native Ecuador when he was two years old. They had struggled for years to have their own biological children and had emptied half their life savings with multiple rounds of *in vitro* fertilization and other extraordinary measures. When they finally concluded that God was leading them to adopt, they emptied the rest of their life savings in the insanely expensive adoption process.[8]

Jim and Susan were referred to me by their pediatrician, who had a hunch that Danny had been misdiagnosed when he was five. He was struggling in school, but was otherwise a respectful, responsible young man. He had a fantastic sense of humor, which included a healthy sarcasm that became part of our weekly repartee. We started each session with a series of put-downs, which tended to put us both at ease and prepared us for the serious work at hand.

Danny's Kindergarten teacher had reported some of the classic ADHD-like symptoms that usually bring children to the pediatrician: overactivity (whatever that means), difficulty sitting still, fidgeting, an inability to settle down for quiet activities, not listening when he was spoken to, and tantrums when confronted or scolded. His parents, believing they were being responsible and loving, immediately brought Danny to a highly recommended child psychologist for an evaluation.

Within an hour, the psychologist gave a preliminary diagnosis of ADHD, Hyperactive-Impulsive Type. He recommended a full evaluation, including rating scales completed by parents and his teacher.

---

7   One example is Wilson Reading. Tutors trained in this research-based, multi-sensory technique often results in vastly improved phonological processing, fluency, and reading comprehension.

8   When I become king, adoption will be made free to all deserving parents.

The evaluator also had Danny try a computer test that supposedly measured his ability to maintain attention.

Not surprisingly, the rating scales supported the ADHD diagnosis. The psychologist performed no medical tests and made no effort to rule out other problems that often manifest in ADHD-like behaviors. When the parents suggested that their son's difficulties might be related to his adoption, the psychologist pooh-poohed the idea. They relented, feeling that they should implicitly trust his judgment. By the end of the week, Jim and Susan were at the pharmacy with a prescription for Adderall.

Danny's brain did not like Adderall. He became manic within hours, literally bouncing off the walls, screaming constantly, whipping around like a whirling dervish. He could not sit still for *anything*. He was constantly irate, ecstatic, or weeping. His parents wisely stopped the Adderall immediately. They tried lowering the dose—which was already relatively low. While this reduced the awful side effects, the drug now did absolutely nothing to help.

Danny's brain did not like Concerta, which gave him awful tics and made him zombie-like at school. The teacher, who had initially complained about Danny's ADHD-like behavior, was now wishing she had the "old Danny" back. Danny's brain did not particularly like Strattera, either. Although it had few side effects, it did absolutely nothing for his behavior in school. In fact, his First Grade teacher suggested that Danny might have a learning disability, not ADHD.

Jim and Susan then had Danny evaluated by the school. The school psychologist tested his abilities, which were determined to be average. His reading, on the other hand, was determined to be weak; Danny's reading speed was slow, while his ability to sound out words was relatively poor. His new diagnosis was Dyslexia (Reading Disorder). Soon, Danny was in a special daily reading group.

Danny loathed reading. He avoided it at school, dragging his feet whenever asked to read in class. He threw a fit at home when asked to read, and often dug in his heels during homework time whenever reading was involved. Anytime he read, he squinted and said that his eyes were tired. Schoolwork became such a struggle over the next few years that the whole family dynamic soured. The three to four hour period after school was renamed "wartime" and the kitchen table where he was supposed to complete homework was dubbed the "western front."

Danny and his parents came to me with little hope for any success. The parents admitted to me, "We've been to our share of psychologists and psychiatrists, and no one has been able to help us." I asked about the family structure, which, on the surface, seemed appropriate. Mom and Dad firmly believed that they were in charge. They seemed to have reasonable limits and expectations of Danny, including adequate school performance.

On a hunch, I asked whether Danny had had a full vision screening. Although he had had the school's vision screening, he had never had a fuller evaluation. I explained that children who complain of tired eyes and squint often are simply avoiding an unpopular task; however, some actually struggle to focus on letters and words, which is both physically and emotionally uncomfortable. I recommended a full visual evaluation with a developmental optometrist.

The evaluator determined that Danny had significant convergence insufficiency, something that would not show up on a school vision screening. Essentially, his eye muscles were not strong enough to hold the focus necessary for reading and Mathematics—any tasks that required scanning symbols in a sequence. Because of this visual weakness, his eyes avoided scanning tasks like reading, which resulted in the series of behaviors that teachers, parents, and psychologists misinterpreted as ADHD, Learning Disability, and the dreaded Lazy Butt Disorder.

Luckily, convergence insufficiency did not require surgery or a lifetime of therapy. It simply required some visual exercises that he could do at home. In 10 weeks, Danny was no longer squinting. He was able to focus his eyes far better and for longer periods of time. The consequence was striking. He was now not only able to read for longer periods of time; he was devouring books like a kid who was making his first visit to a candy store. His attention problems in school disappeared.

Danny spent our final session reading to me from my favorite book, *Lord of the Rings*. He even used a laughable but precious British accent. At the end, I asked him, "So where did your disability go?" Without skipping a beat, he answered, "I never had one. I just had disabled doctors." From the mouths of babes…

Chapter 5
What Children Can and Should Expect in Return for Being Good Citizens

Fathers, do not exasperate your children, so that they will not lose heart.

~Colossians 3:21

You may be deceived if you trust too much,
but you will live in torment if you do not trust enough.

~Frank Crane

Forced Volunteerism

"Why should I work my butt off in school if I don't get anything out of it? My parents never let me do anything. What's the point?"

Michelle was, by all accounts, a parent's dream. In addition to being a highly successful student who had recently been accepted to Princeton, Berkeley, and MIT, she was an all-state cross-country runner. She had never tried drugs or alcohol, was always respectful, obedient to a fault, and highly responsible. The only problem was that she was miserable. She had just been grounded for a month for sneaking out after bedtime with some of her cross-country friends to tee-pee a friend who was competing in a state gymnastics meet.

"Of course we limit what you can do, Michelle; it's our job to keep you safe and help you get the things you want, like get into a good college, have a good career…"

"I'm almost 18! I'm going to college in seven months and you won't even let me go to prom! You think I'm so stupid that I'm going to wind up pregnant and run away to Virginia or something, skip college and have 14 kids by the time I'm 20!"

"That's not true. You couldn't have 14 kids in two years anyway."

"Tell that to the Octomom. Admit it—you think we'd all use drugs and have wild orgies on prom night."

"Honey, I know what kids do on prom night. I was 18 once too, y'know…"

"I'm not you! I'm tired of being the good girl all the time, doing everything perfect and having nothing to show for it."

"Nothing to show for it?! Your dad and I are so proud of you. And you're going to be at one of the best schools in the country. You have such a bright future ahead of you."

"That's not what I want."

"Tell me, what do you want?"

"Aarrgghh!! I just told you!!!"

Most people can extol the virtues of volunteering. I'm all for it. In fact, I do some *pro bono* work. But most people can't pay their bills by volunteering or giving away their time and services for free. You need to be paid for what you do, or your motivation to work will shrink as fast as your wallet.

Children are no different. They need to know that their efforts will be rewarded. We are, after all, creatures of reward. If they are not sufficiently rewarded for being safe, respectful, obedient, and doing their share of work, then they will certainly not put forth great effort toward these endeavors. So what motivates children to follow the Four Expectations? What do they get in return? What do they really want?

I believe that almost all rewards boil down to these four categories: respect, trust, freedom, and privileges. These are the rewards that Parents in Charge eagerly offer their children, when they are earned.

Respect

For children, the most important reinforcers are social; they do not involve tangible things like money or stickers. The most potent social reinforcer is respect. As I discussed in Chapter Two, all children have a right to a certain level of respect. But children who behave respectfully, obey my rules, perform their fair share of work, and behave safely will earn a higher level of respect from me than those who fail to meet the Four Expectations.

How do Parents in Charge offer respect to their children? First, they pay attention to them. One of the most fundamental ways to withhold respect from someone is to ignore them. Imagine speaking to someone who simply turns away, ignores you, looks at their watch, or walks away from you. How deflating! Now imagine someone you love deeply attentive to you, putting aside all distractions to focus her attention solely on you, giving you eye contact, nodding as you talk, reflecting back to you so that you know you are heard.

Your children desire your attention. Even the adolescent who often seems to desire anything *but* your presence craves moments of your rapt, undivided attention. When you pay attention to your child, she feels loved, cared for, understood, and valued. You communicate to her that she is worthwhile. But this kind of deep attention must be given only in response to sufficient respect.

Here's an example. Your twelve-year-old informs you Saturday afternoon that he invited his friend Jimmy for a sleepover that night. He didn't ask you; he just did it on his own. Your response should be something like, "Nope." End of discussion; do not even consider allowing it. However, if he comes to you and says, "Mom, Dad, can we discuss inviting Jimmy for a sleepover tonight?" then you should reward him for the superbly respectful way he asked you permission by paying close attention to his request. You might still say no, but you honor his respect toward you by reflecting it back to him.

Second, Parents in Charge reward their respectful children with the same level of verbal discourse they desire from their children. They do not yell, scream, cuss, patronize, mock, mimic, make the "you have the IQ of a kumquat" face, or belittle their children. Also, they do not reject requests out-of-hand, but consider them thoughtfully. Now, I'm not saying that if your child is rude or gnarly with you that you should be rude and gnarly in response. You simply will not entertain any discussions with a rude or gnarly child.

The third way we respect our children involves affection. Hugs, kisses (yes, even teenagers need hugs and kisses), high-fives, pats on the back, backrubs, back scratches, and so on, are perfectly healthy, normal, appropriate gestures of love and respect. Parents in Charge don't offer backrubs to children who just threw a tantrum or who just refused to pick up their clothes. Rather, they wait for an apology and the clothes to be picked up; then comes the nice backrub.

Offering and providing a child age-appropriate privacy reflects a great deal of respect. While also a reflection of trust, it strongly motivates children, particularly as they get older. As with other areas of respect, some privacy should be afforded all children, such as their bodies, thoughts, and feelings.

Trust

Your children want to be trusted. They need to know that you find them worthy of your trust. How do children desire to be trusted?

- Younger children say "I want to do it myself!" when they want to be trusted to express their independence with tasks. When your young child is able to get dressed without help, he wants you to *trust* him to do so.
- One of the most important developmental tasks of school-age children is growing the sense of capability in doing age-appropriate things. This includes a million things like homework, cooking, mowing the lawn, screwing in a light

bulb, figuring out how to use gadgets, and taking care of a pet. Children feel an enormous sense of empowerment and self-value when you trust them to do these things.

- For teenagers, one of the biggest areas of trust involves driving. Imagine your child turning 16 and wanting to drive a car. Will you trust your teen or will you need every fiber of self-control to hide the panic attack that bubbles under the surface? Be sure, your adolescent will desire your trust and will resent you if you do not seem eager to offer it.

- Your children desire your trust regarding their choice of friends of both sexes. They want to know that you trust their discernment and ability to set and maintain boundaries with others. This becomes increasingly important as your children enter the teenage years and desire special relationships with the opposite sex.

Trusting Your Child in the Big Bad World

Recall Michelle from the beginning of this chapter. Her mother was struggling mightily with trusting Michelle, even though she had hardly given her any reason to distrust her. When pressed, her mother agreed that Michelle was worthy of a great level of trust. She admitted, however, that her distrust did not stem from Michelle, but from her experience with the rest of the world and modern culture.

Michelle's mother admitted to her that she had gotten pregnant when she was 19, during her first year of college. She had an abortion and became deeply depressed, quitting school for two years before returning to complete her B.A. She admitted regretting so much of her past and worrying constantly that her daughter would "follow in my horrible footsteps."

Over time, Michelle's mother was able to recognize that much of her fear was irrational—that Michelle was as responsible and wise as any adult she knew. She also practiced accurate thinking about her daughter: she raised her quite well and her sphere of influence in her life was waning. She became more comfortable believing that this was a good, natural thing. With this growing sense, she was able to put aside her irrational fears and allow her daughter the trust that she deserved—and needed to develop.

Freedom

One of the biggest rewards your child craves is freedom. Your child wants freedom to do things she could not previously do, freedom to go places she has not been allowed, and freedom to speak and behave in a more adult or equal manner. Some of these freedoms should be available to your child when he or she shows excellent safety, obedience, and respect and when he or she is old enough.

For example, my nine-year-old daughter is essentially safe, obedient, and respectful. She wants to be able to ride her bike across the street to her friend's house. Because she has proven that she can do so safely, we now allow her to do this.

An obedient and safe child should be free to choose which clothes he or she will wear to school and most other places and events. Obviously, you don't allow your child to go outside in freezing weather with bermuda shorts on, but if your daughter wants to go to the grocery store wearing plaid golf pants with a polyester disco shirt, leave her alone. You've heard of picking your battles; I implore you to stop picking this battle.[9] Remember, Parents in Charge aren't control freaks. They only control safety, respect, obedience, and work.

Similarly, Parents in Charge allow children to structure their own free time. I see parents making the mistake of trying to fill every moment of their child's life with "positive, growth-oriented experiences," including those precious moments of down-time after homework and chores are done. "Shouldn't you study for your test a little more?" Well, actually, no. What Junior really needs is some time to just sit there and contemplate his navel for a while. If he's done his chores and homework, leave him alone. He might be figuring out cold fusion or the meaning of life. He doesn't need his parents interrupting.

Of course, there are certain limits to freedom that have nothing to do with how safe, respectful, obedient, or hard-working your child is. No matter how mature your child, it remains your job as parents to place limits that ensure his or her safety. For example, I am not allowing my children to go to heavy metal concerts when they are 13. I don't care how mature my child is; it's just not safe or appropriate for a 13-year-old. When my daughters are 16, I will not let her date

---

9   Because one's dress reflects one's attitude, there should be some basic limitations regarding what your child wears to school and places of worship.

a 22-year-old. That's sick and wrong regardless of how respectful, obedient, and responsible she is!

One of the other freedoms Parents in Charge allow their adolescents to earn is the right to speak to them in a more adult-to-adult manner. Eventually, you would like to interact with your adult child as more of a peer. While you will always hold a place of honor and respect in her life, you recognize that you will someday have to release the mantle of authority. When your adolescent shows superb respect, safety, responsibility, and work ethic, you can begin speaking to your adolescent like an adult. Most adolescents prize this privilege.

Privileges

Remember the list of privileges from Chapter Two? Those are tangible things your child greatly desires. Your child will be even more motivated by them if he must work for them—if they are not simply given with the aim of making your child happy or getting him to like you. By definition, privileges are *earned* things or activities that reinforce positive behavior.

Video games are an excellent example of a privilege. For many children, this highly reinforcing activity can induce them to do just about anything. I remember one 11-year-old who had been struggling to clean his room pleading with his mother, "Please, I'll clean the entire house if you just let me play one hour on my Wii!" His mom negotiated him down to a daily five-minute room clean and a post-dinner table-clear in order to earn his Wii for a half hour daily and an hour on weekends. He was a happy camper; mom was a happier camper.

To others, the sleepover[10] represents the grand prize. "You want a sleepover? Fine. Gimme two straight weeks of 100% homework completion, no test grades below C, and a spotless room every evening by 7 PM and you've got yourself a sleepover with pizza and all the movies you can stay awake for." It's really amazing what kids will do when they really want something that must be earned.

Dessert should usually be treated as a privilege—for children and adults. As I discussed in Chapter Three, you cannot maintain absolute control over how much your children eat or what they eat outside the

---

10 More appropriately dubbed the "Stay-up-all-night-and-be-crabby-for-the-next-two-days-Over"

home. You can be in control of your children's food choices and whether or not your children get dessert. Hard-fast rules won't work here. For some, eating vegetables and a portion of the other foods earns dessert. For others, eating half of everything does the job. Some parents are "plate-cleaners"—leaving any crumb on the plate is strictly *verboten*! Vee vill not vaste food!

I think two choices make sense. The best choice makes dessert a rarity in the first place, thereby striking the whole dessert chapter out of the dinner drama. The next best choice is to put only the food on the plate that your child is expected to eat in order to get dessert. This reduces game-playing and manipulating. You would never again hear, "How many more bites of this do I have to eat to get ice cream?"

Of course, one of the biggest motivators and rewards—especially for older children and adolescents—is money. Cold, hard cash. Not money in the bank to be used for college education. That doesn't do it for kids and teens. Whether you call it allowance or a paycheck or something else, your child values dollars just as you do.

Why should you pay your child to be safe, respectful, obedient, and do his work? Three reasons. First, it works as a great motivator. Second, because children need to learn how to deal with money; paying them will help them learn to appreciate, use, and save money. Third, because it mirrors the real-life scenario of a career. When you perform the duties of your job, you receive compensation. When you do not perform the duties satisfactorily, you do not get paid or you get fired.[11] Following this pattern early on sets a template for your child: he must work hard to get what he wants.

Question: how much should you pay your child to do what he or she should be doing anyway, like helping around the house? Answer: just enough that your child can enjoy the fruits of his labor, but not so much that he doesn't need to earn it frequently. If you pay him too much, he won't need the money next week and his motivation to earn will decrease. Essentially, you want your child to live paycheck to paycheck, so that he needs to work to enjoy the lifestyle he desires.

---

11 Fortunately, we cannot fire our children.

Learn your Child's Reinforcement Profile

Parents in Charge communicate with their children regarding what will be rewarding to them. They avoid the mistake of rewarding their children with respect, trust, freedoms, and privileges that are not earned or not even desired. Similarly, they work hard to give their children enough of these to satisfy their sense of fairness. Remember, if your children perceive that they are not getting their fair share of respect, trust, freedom, and privileges, you will soon find them as unmotivated to meet the Four Expectations as Michelle was.

Chapter 6
The Family Constitution

What's done to children, they will do to society.

~Karl Menninger

No matter how calmly you try to referee, parenting will eventually produce bizarre behavior, and I'm not talking about the kids.

~Bill Cosby

The Document

By now, you understand the basics. First, you understand the necessity of a proper family hierarchy in a family's overall health. Second, you are committed to creating and maintaining your position as a Parent in Charge. Third, you comprehend the difference between rights and privileges. Fourth, you understand the Four Expectations you must have for your children. Finally, you know which rewards are most effective in getting your children to meet those expectations.

Any good system of government has a constitution. The *American Heritage Dictionary* defines a constitution as "the system of fundamental laws and principles that prescribes the nature, functions, and limits of a government or another institution." It also refers to the document that describes the system. You are ready to formalize the changes to your family by creating your own **Family Constitution**.

Your Family Constitution does not need to be as formal sounding as the following. You can create it any way you like, but for now, a formal sounding document can support the serious tone you need to take. You can use the **Family Constitution Worksheet** at the end of this book (Appendix A) to work on your own Family Constitution.

Preamble:

Here you will spell out the purpose of your Family Constitution. You will establish the design and significance of your family. You will also list the vision and overarching goals that you have set for your family. Go ahead and sound formal and lofty; remember, you are founding a great institution that will achieve great things.

Example:

We the Smith Family, *in order to form a more perfect Union, establish justice, insure peace in our home, provide for all our needs, promote the development of all family members, and to teach godly principles and knowledge, do ordain and establish this Constitution for our family.*

Section One: The Structure of your Family:

First, you must establish who is in charge. Explain why you are in charge. Feel free to refer to God, the government, and common sense.

Inform your children of their position in the family. Why are they not equal partners? What is the relationship between Mom and Dad? What role does Grandma have? Who holds the mantle of authority when Mom and Dad are not around? Establish the hierarchy.

Example:

Mom and Dad are the leaders and originators of this family. Their authority stems from several sources, including God and common sense, as well as their superior knowledge and wisdom in caring for this family. The governments of our city and state also support Mom and Dad's authority.

Both Mom and Dad are equal authorities in this family. Dad maintains final say in most matters, because there are times when one person will need to make a final decision about difficult things. However, Mom's say is equal to Dad's; when Dad is not present, all rules and expectations must be followed as if Dad were there. The same applies when Mom is not present. Furthermore, all respect owed to one parent is also owed to the other; any disrespect shown toward one parent will be perceived as disrespect toward both parents. Grandma and Grandpa possess authority in all matters when Mom and Dad are not present. The family rules fully apply; they have authority to enforce the rules.

When Jenna, Alex, and Susan are by themselves—either downstairs or outside—none of them is in charge of the others. For example, Jenna does not have authority over Alex and Susan. However, because of her older age, she has more responsibility and can remind either sibling of the rules and possible consequences. It is not her job to discipline the others; in fact, she may not discipline her siblings.[12]

Section Two: Rights and Privileges

Your children need to be aware of your commitment to providing for their needs. At the same time, they need to comprehend the shift in policy regarding privileges. No longer will they reap the full complement of privileges without sowing the proper seeds. Now they must earn whatever privileges they desire. At the same time, they must recognize that you will unconditionally care for their basic needs. Remember,

---

12 At some point, you should specify what one child should do in response to a misbehaving sibling. Explain the difference between tattling for revenge and informing parents in order to help keep that sibling safe.

you *love* your children unconditionally but you do not *express* your love unconditionally!

Example:

Because Mom and Dad love their children unconditionally, there are certain rights that all children will have in this family:
- *Love*
- *Protection*
- *Valid, fair discipline*
- *Rules and expectations will be clear and fully explained*
- *Freedom of religion*
- *Freedom of speech*
- *Food, clothing, shelter*
- *Freedom of thought*
- *Freedom to feel*
- *Be informed about medical issues and treatments*
- *Privacy*
- *Sexual integrity*
- *No physical abuse or misuse*
- *No emotional abuse or bullying*

Mom and Dad are committed to respecting all of these rights. All other privileges must be earned. These privileges are described in Section Four of this Constitution.

Parents in Charge also have rights! It makes sense to clarify these with your children.

Example:

Mom and Dad also have rights. Mom and Dad have the right to:
- *Verbal and physical respect*
- *Have their possessions respected*
- *Consult with other parents and professionals about parenting challenges*
- *Establish their authority in the family and household*
- *Decide meals*
- *Privacy (purses, wallets, dresser drawers, do not enter parents' room without first knocking, etc.)*

- *Downtime (not to be bothered after 9 PM, except in case of emergency)*
- *Choose the music in the house or in the car*

Respecting these rights is non-negotiable.

Section Three: The Four Major Expectations

1. Safety
2. Respect
3. Obedience
4. Work

Establish what each of these means in your house. Be specific—very specific. Do not hesitate to explain the importance of each. Introduce the notion that meeting expectations will result in rewards.

Example:

The children must adhere to four major expectations; almost all rules fall under these four categories. If they follow these expectations, they will earn not only Mom and Dad's respect, but will also earn appropriate freedoms and privileges.

The first and most important expectation is to **BE SAFE***. This means your safety, the safety of your family, and the safety of the home. Specifically, this means that drug use and/or possession will not be tolerated. Drug paraphernalia will also not be allowed. This includes cigarettes. There will be no compromise on this expectation. Drinking alcohol will be allowed on special occasions only with parental permission, supervision, and limits.*

All family members are expected to take reasonable care of themselves. This means that you will not engage in unreasonably high-risk behaviors. Whitewater rafting, paintball, roller coasters, and parasailing are not included (Mom and Dad might even drag you along with us when we do them!). Music concerts that are likely to involve drug use, "mosh pits", or otherwise questionable activities will be deemed unsafe.[13]

---

13 Some of the items in a Constitution would be overkill for younger children. You don't need to tell your five-year-old to say no to drugs. You shouldn't need to tell them not to be serial murderers, either. If you think you do, give me a call—we need to talk.

*The second expectation is to **BE RESPECTFUL**. All family members are expected to respect all other family members, including parents, siblings, grandparents, aunts, uncles, and cousins. Respect means:*

Verbal respect: *speaking kindly in word and tone both to and about family members.*
Verbal respect includes appropriate manners:
- *Responding when spoken to*
- *Maintaining eye contact during conversation*
- *Validating another's perspective or feelings*
- *Saying "please" and "thank you" and other niceties*
- *Offering genuine compliments*
- *Constructive criticism*
- *Saying "Yes, Mom" or "OK, Dad" in response to a command*
- *Maintaining self-controlled voice during debate/argument*
- *Taking responsibility for one's mistakes and apologizing*

Some examples of disrespect are:
- *Rolling eyes when spoken to*
- *Saying loudly, "I know!"*
- *Defying (saying "No!" to a command)*
- *Lying*
- *Correcting adults in a challenging, unloving way*
- *Not looking at adults when spoken to*
- *"Storming" out of the room: huffing and puffing sighs, stomping*
- *Destructive criticism*

Physical respect: *respecting the personal space of others*
Some examples of disrespect are:
- *Excessive, unwelcome affection (bear hugs, tickling, kissing)*
- *Uninvited wrestling, boxing, and other forms of aggressive play*
- *Spitting*

Respect of property: *Maintaining the safety and privacy of others' things and room*

Some examples are:

- *Not going in siblings' room without permission (for older children/teens)*
- *Not touching "special" belongings (e.g., iPod, diary) without permission*
- *Stealing*
- *Not defacing or otherwise damaging others' things*
- *Respecting the cars by not messing them*

Respect of your body: *Taking reasonable care of yourself*
- *Maintaining sound hygiene*
- *Going to sleep at a reasonable hour*
- *Following physicians' orders, such as medication and other treatments*

*The third and related expectation demands that children **OBEY THE RULES**. While there are many rules in our home and some specific rules may change from time to time, most of the general rules always apply. Primarily, we expect you to do what you are told/requested/commanded to do immediately and without argument, complaint, or dawdling. We do not expect you to immediately stop something you are doing if it requires finishing steps (for example, if you have to save a computer game or finish writing a sentence); in this case, you may say, "OK Mom, I'm just finishing this sentence/saving the game; I'll do it right away." If you abuse this by consistently dragging out the completion of activities in order to avoid doing what was requested, we will then begin to expect you to drop everything immediately.*

Mom and Dad agree to avoid asking you to do things when you are in the middle of a task or fun activity. Sometimes our requests can wait. However, sometimes they cannot and we will make it clear that we expect you to comply immediately with our command. For example, if Mom is in the bathroom and you are in the middle of a television program and the phone rings, you might be told to answer the phone. This cannot wait and we expect you to leave the television and answer the phone.

One important rule is keeping your room clean. All bedrooms must have beds made and clothes picked up off the floor before school.

Another important rule involves curfew. You are expected to be home on time, according to the kitchen clock. For every minute that you are late, you will have to be home 10 minutes earlier the next time you go out. In extraordinary circumstances when you cannot get home on time, you must contact Mom or Dad immediately to let us know and collaborate on a plan for getting you home as soon as possible.

*The fourth expectation is to **DO YOUR WORK**. This includes both schoolwork and chores. All children go to school to prepare for their career and to learn the fundamentals of life. We expect you to work hard in this endeavor. To this end, we have the following expectations:*

- *You must attend school every day. The only exceptions will be when you are significantly ill. Sniffles don't count.*
- *You must complete all homework satisfactorily (neatly and according to your teachers' expectations). You must hand it in on time.*
- *You must complete your homework independently and in your room. Mom and Dad will be available as much as possible to help with any questions you may have, but we will not complete work for you under any circumstances. If we are not available, you remain responsible to get the help you need. You may contact other students or go to school early. It is not Mom and Dad's job to rescue you from any mistakes you make, including forgetting books, assignments, or any other materials you might need. If the school places unrealistic expectations on you, we will intervene on your behalf.*
- *You may listen to music while you do homework, as long as you earn that freedom by performing your work satisfactorily. However, you may not have the TV or computer on while doing homework, unless you are using the computer to complete the assignment.*
- *You are all intelligent and able enough to achieve C's or better on all tests and quizzes. We expect you to achieve A's or B's, but understand that some subjects or classes might be particularly challenging.*
- *We expect you to behave like good citizens in the classroom, giving your teachers and other students respect and following all appropriate school rules. If there are any rules you feel are not*

appropriate, you must first discuss this with Mom and Dad and get permission from them to break the rule.[14]

Mom and Dad work hard to take care of this family, both financially and in the upkeep of our home. Because we expect you to help with these, we have developed daily and weekly chores for you to perform. These are your home jobs. We expect you to complete your chores daily before you enjoy any of the privileges you enjoy. Similarly, you are expected to complete your weekend chore before you go anywhere or enjoy any of your privileges. We are committed to being flexible with your busy schedule, not giving you chores when you are not home for long enough to be expected to complete them.

Section Four: The Four Rewards

Describe what your response will be to your children following the Four Expectations: what will they get out of it, how you will feel about it.

We are confident that all of our children will be able to maintain their safety, respect one another, obey Mom and Dad, and perform their work adequately. We are committed to making these expectations as rewarding as possible. When you are adequately meeting the Four Expectations, you will earn the following:

1. *Our respect*

   - *We will be more likely to be pleasant and affectionate with you.*[15]
   - *We will pay attention to you.*
   - *It will be far easier to consider your requests.*
   - *We will also give you as much privacy as is safe.*

---

14 While Parents in Charge generally defer to school authority and encourage respect and obedience, some school rules/expectations are so foolish that they invite civil disobedience. Example: being expected to participate in a mock worship service for a religion different from that which your family practices.

15 For teenagers, you may add "but not in public". If you and your teen appreciate humor, go ahead and add "<u>especially</u> in public."

2. *Trust*

- *We will trust you to walk to the next block by yourself (with friends).*[16]
- *You may keep a private diary that Mom and Dad will not look at except in case of emergencies.*
- *We will not doubt your word.*

3. *Freedom*

- *(For girls) You may wear makeup for special occasions.*
- *You may choose your own clothes (subject to parental approval, of course)*
- *You may ride your bike or walk to school on your own or with friends.*
- *You may have access to your own bank account.*
- *You may spend your money as you choose (within reason, of course).*

4. *Privileges*

- *We will give you an allowance of $10 per week, half of which will be placed in a savings account for your college education. One dollar will be given to church as an offering.*[17] *You may spend the remaining $4 on anything you wish.*
- *We will allow you to have friends over on weekends.*
- *You will be able to buy and use a cell phone (when you are 14).*
- *You may play video games for a half hour per day after your chores and homework are done satisfactorily.*
- *You may watch TV for a half hour per day, after your chores and homework are complete.*
- *You may use your iPod during homework*[18] *or when you are out.*

---

16 For older teenagers, this area of trust will pertain to driving or using public transportation.

17 Or whatever amount you decide for each child. If your family does not go to church or synagogue, they can give the dollar to a local charity. The point is instilling the idea of regular giving and service.

18 For older children who have already proven their ability to complete work with music playing.

- *You may have a sleepover during vacations (like Christmas or Spring Break).*

Describe what your response will be if they do not follow these expectations. You don't need to be specific here; sometimes the unknown can keep them on their toes.

Example:

Mistakes are part of the learning and growing process; we expect you to make plenty of them. Our job as parents will be to respond to these mistakes in a way that trains you to learn from your mistakes and to make better choices in the future. Just as it would be foolish to pay an employee who does not complete his work, we will not pay you (offer you the Four Rewards) when you do not do your job (meet the Four Expectations). However, we will be ready and eager to reestablish those rewards as you meet the Four Expectations.

The primary method of training will be to withhold your "paycheck." You will earn less Trust, Respect, Freedom, and Privileges. Of course, minor mistakes will result in smaller consequences or fines. Major mistakes, such as gross disrespect, unsafe behavior, or defiance, will result in an automatic, near-complete withdrawal of rewards. Mom and Dad will specify the rewards and consequences in a separate, more flexible document.

Chapter 7

There'll Be a Test on Friday: How to Enact Your Family Constitution

If you have never been hated by your child, you have never been a parent.

~Bette Davis

I don't believe professional athletes should be role models. I believe parents should be role models.... It's not like it was when I was growing up. My mom and my grandmother told me how it was going to be. If I didn't like it, they said, "Don't let the door hit you in the ass on your way out." Parents have to take better control.

~Charles Barkley

Now What?

Congratulations! You have joined the ranks of the illustrious by creating your very own **Family Constitution**. Make sure you use a font that looks official and you leave space for all family members to sign your founding document. Remember, you are the Founding Father and Mother of this great family. Eat your hearts out, John Adams and Thomas Jefferson.

After a bit of self-congratulatory celebration, you will ask yourself, "OK, now what?" You likely know U.S. history well enough to know that just because the founders established a constitution, there was no assurance that the colonies would ratify it. There was a lot of work, negotiating, bickering, explaining, and convincing that ensued. You too must effectively communicate the brilliance of your Family Constitution to your children so that they not only see its wisdom, but also comprehend how beneficial it can be for them.

Pick a time and place to begin

Your children might perceive some of the rumblings of change that are afoot. They may have seen *Desperately Seeking Parents* lying around the house, dog-eared. They may have heard some conversations about limits, rights, privileges, chores, or intolerance for disrespect. They might be scared. The first thing to realize is that change is scary. Even positive change.

Stress essentially represents any change to a system. Changing the hierarchy of your family and altering the expectations you have for your children will represent major stresses for all family members. Relegating those things that used to be rights to their proper place as privileges will place a significant stress on your family. Mom and Dad uniting and communicating more often might signal a major change for your children (and for you). Another potential stress will come when you no longer (inadvertently) reinforce negative behavior patterns. More about that later.

It is a good idea to announce to the children that you are working on some family changes. Set up a time to meet when everyone will be present; stress the importance of all family members comprehending the changes. Tell your children to come prepared to listen, to ask questions, and to offer their opinion (respectfully, of course).

One word of advice, which is always wise for meetings that carry potential for stress: bring goodies. Have donuts, ice cream, or chocolate, whatever your family likes. Sure, it's pandering, but so what? You're asking them to participate in a massive shift of power. A tasty peace offering can ease the pain. Of course, it is a well-known scientific fact that stressful information is easier to digest in combination with a bowl of peanut butter chocolate ice cream.

Read the Family Constitution Together

Once your flock has migrated to the meeting place, make sure the Parents in Charge sit together. This reflects your show of unity, which is essential to the following task. Hand out copies of the Family Constitution to each member of the family (unless the child isn't old enough to read). One parent should be the spokesperson. Begin by saying something along these lines:

> Thank you all for being here today. This is a very important meeting because Mom and Dad are going to be explaining some big changes in our home. As you may know, there have been some difficulties in our family for a long time. We are not going to spend a lot of time talking about that tonight. We are here tonight to talk about the positive changes we will be making.

> You can see that you all have a copy of a document called *Our Family Constitution*. I am going to read it out loud to you so that you all know what is coming soon. Nothing is going to change right away. We are simply going to let you know what the tentative plan is, have time for questions and concerns, and then open the floor to suggestions. If you think of something after this meeting, feel free to mention it to Mom or Dad in the next couple days, so we can listen and consider your suggestions before we complete the final, official version of this document.

> We will be implementing these changes one week from tonight. We will have one more meeting to go over all of

this again. We don't want any of you to be in the dark, so make sure you are here.

Then go ahead and read the Family Constitution, from the beginning. Do not entertain questions until you have completed the whole thing. Then open the floor to questions. Ask your children if there are any suggestions they might have for the Four Rewards. Let them know that you as the Parents in Charge are committed to making this work for everyone in your family—that you want all family members to be successful in earning all of the available privileges. Specifically, let them know that they have the opportunity to earn even more trust, respect, freedom, and privileges that they had been enjoying in the past.

Wise parents take the important, humble step of admitting their mistakes to their children. Admitting that you have erred by rewarding bad behavior, treating privileges as rights, and failing to act as united parents can go a long way to role modeling for your children the need to make changes. If you're not sure you can muster up that kind of humility for your children, work on it. It's important. Practice saying, "We have been wrong." I promise, it won't kill you.

When you discuss your Family Constitution, be sure to use the phrase "Mom and Dad" (or vice-versa) as often as possible. You don't need to spend much time on the issue of whether Mom or Dad ultimately assumes the role of family leader. Mom and Dad together comprise the Parents in Charge. You have united to parent your children; that is all that matters for now.

A Week of Warnings

Because you are initiating a quantum shift in your parenting, it is wise to consider the week between the first and second conversation as a trial run. During that week, Mom and Dad should have daily conversations about expectations and rewards. Ask yourselves:

1. Which of the Four Expectations did my child meet today that we could reinforce?
2. How can we reinforce that? Which of the Four Rewards would fit and to what degree?

3. Which of the Four Expectations did my child not meet that would not earn some of the Four Rewards?

4. What behaviors are difficult for us to judge (whether they fall under the Four Expectations)? Can we come to some agreement or compromise about this?

Make lists of the first two and communicate them to your child. Tell him or her which behaviors were great and will definitely earn some of the Four Rewards when things get started. Conversely, inform him or her which behaviors will definitely not be tolerated. Offer some hint as to what consequences will ensue if such behaviors continue after the Constitution goes into effect the following week.

You might be surprised to find there are several behavioral patterns that are quite bothersome to one parent but the other parent finds tolerable or even acceptable. Negotiate this between yourselves; take your time.[19] Write down whatever decision you make, because you will communicate it at the following meeting. This is critical to your success, because if one parent does not agree with certain expectations, the authority expressed through rewards and consequences will be too weak to make a difference. Unity is paramount!

Meet Again to Review the Basics and Entertain Questions

A week later, sit the children down again and go over the Family Constitution. You don't need to read it again, but if you all want to take turns reading it, fine. Make sure your children have the opportunity to ask questions, offer their opinions, and share any feelings they have about the upcoming changes. You will likely hear some complaint or confusion as to why you are making the changes. Just listen and tell them you understand their concerns, and explain to them that you have made mistakes in the past and are working to improve your parenting.

---

19 If you struggle to negotiate the Four Expectations and Four Rewards on your own, consider consulting with an objective third party. First choice: another couple whose parenting you respect. Second choice: a professional who specializes in family therapy and who emphasizes a parents-first philosophy.

Have Each Family Member Sign the Family Constitution

After fielding all questions, comments, and suggestions, have each child sign the Family Constitution. Remind them that their signature does not indicate that they agree with every part of the Constitution—or any of it, for that matter—but that they understand it. They are acknowledging that you have informed them about the changes, so that there can be no future "You never told me…" episodes.

Inform your children that your Family Constitution is in full effect starting today. Inform them that you will meet again in a week or so to entertain questions, comments, and discuss how things are working.

You're in business!

Expect a Behavior "Spike"

"OK, Dr. P., you said that if I stopped rewarding Jenny's tantrums by talking to her and giving in, she would stop the tantrums. Well, it's been three days. I've been ignoring her, but her tantrums are worse, thank you very much. Is this one of those 'worse before it gets better' things?"

In my work, making mistakes can have disastrous consequences. And because I have a healthy-sized ego, I would rather submit to some bizarre medieval torture device than admit my mistakes. As much as I hated admitting my mistake with Jenny and her Mom, I had to fess up. I had neglected to warn her sufficiently about the behavior spike.

I would be remiss if I did not admit that after you implement your Family Constitution, things might indeed get worse before they get better. Here a lesson from Psychology 101 can help us understand why.

Psychologists with nothing better to do but use grant money did some really interesting experiments with pigeons. The pigeons had nothing better to do either. They signed up for these experiments, most likely figuring they would get a free lunch. The lab-coat doctors designed an experiment where the pigeons had to peck a lever in their cage in order to get a piece of food. As you would guess, the pigeons figured this out rather quickly and began regularly pecking the level whenever they wanted some food. The learned behavior was pecking the lever. The reward was the food. Simple enough.

Then the researchers got mean. They decided to stop rewarding (reinforcing) the pigeons for pecking the lever. They wanted to see what happened. Would they keep pecking? Would they stop? Would they grab pitchforks and torches and march to the dean's office?

Well, what happened was fascinating. The pigeons at first began pecking wildly at the lever, presumably convinced that they must not have pecked often or firmly enough to secure the reinforcement. They continued this for a while, and then gave up. Occasionally they returned for one weak peck, but as long as reinforcement was scarce, the pecking behavior remained extinguished. Gone.

I'm not suggesting that your children are as dumb as pigeons; I'm sure they're all Harvard-bound, full-scholarship material. However, they are like pigeons at least in one respect. When you cease reinforcing or rewarding a certain behavior, you will likely see an increase or "spike" in that behavior for a short time. You can anticipate that your children will intensify their misbehaviors for a short time to secure the reinforcements to which they are accustomed. Even though you warned them that they would no longer be reinforced or rewarded for inappropriate behavior, the reality will take a while to sink in.

If you stand firm as a parental unit, consistently avoid reinforcing the behavior during this spike, and only reinforce your child when he meets the Four Expectations, the negative behaviors will extinguish. Your child will settle into a new way of behaving and relating with you. For some children, this can happen in hours or a few days; with other children—particularly those with more entrenched patterns—you should expect to wait a couple weeks to see the behaviors significantly extinguish.

Hand Out Constitution Grade Cards One Week Later

One week after the start date of the new Constitution, hand out Grade Cards to your children. You can find usable Grade Cards in Appendix C. Feel free to make all the copies you like.

Each child will grade himself or herself on the Four Expectations using a scale of A-F. The grade should reflect their own perception of their performance.

A = Excellent or close to perfect behavior
B = Solid, acceptable, but could still use some work

C = OK, marginal, needs a lot of work, but not horrible
D = Poor, unacceptable behavior
F = Pervasive failure to meet the Four Expectations

They will similarly grade the Parents in Charge on the Four Rewards. These grades pertain to how much trust, respect, freedom, and privileges they have received during that week—<u>not</u> what they deserved.

A=I earned as much as a child my age could receive
B=I received a comfortable level of reward: enough, but not complete
C=I received some reward, but not nearly as much as I would have liked
D=I barely got anything; it was very unpleasant, boring
F=I got nothing; it was like being in jail

Parents should complete their portion together, away from the children. Mom and Dad might disagree on how Junior behaved, partly because Mom and Dad witness different things during the week and have different priorities regarding the children's behavior. This is not the time to air your differences in front of your children. Do not put two separate grades—one for Mom and another for Dad. Instead, have a conference where you listen to each other, compare notes, re-focus on which behavior patterns are problematic, and which positive behaviors would be beneficial to acknowledge.

Junior's Grade Card

Rewards:	Trust	Respect	Freedom	Privileges
Grade:	B+	B	B	D
Grade:	A	B	B	C
Expectations:	Safety	Respect	Obedience	Work

After you each complete your cards, compare the results. Specifically, compare your child's perception of her behavior to your perception of her behavior. Focus on both positive and negative patterns. You must consciously resist two temptations here: focusing solely on negative patterns without noting and reinforcing positive effort and behaviors and ignoring negative behaviors because you want to focus on the positive. Both are crucial. Think of making a good peanut butter and jelly sandwich: you have to have enough of both, but not too much of either.

Mostly likely, you will encounter significant disagreement between you and your child. Do not allow this natural and normal phenomenon to concern you. Remember, your child is learning a new level of acceptable behavior in order to earn what he desires. This represents a significant challenge; human nature inclines him to want to perform minimum work to receive maximum reward.

Still, you may have to reiterate the new order of things. Part of your parental role includes holding the Four Rewards and eagerly meting them out to children who earn them. *Only* when they earn them. It would not be fair, healthy, or good parenting to reward them when they do not meet the expectations. This reflects the arrangement in school and in almost all workplaces. Promise your children that you will work hard to avoid making either mistake of rewarding insufficient behavior or ignoring good behavior.

Meet Two Weeks Later

I know; you have had enough meetings. Still, your family will likely need a refresher course on the expectations and rewards, as well as a review of the specifics of how rewards are determined and meted out. More than likely, your child will have some legitimate complaints:

1. Your daughter finds it unfair for you to hold her accountable for academic work when teachers do not update the website where teachers post grades.
2. Your son reports, "When Dad uses sarcasm or put-downs, it's OK, but when I do it, I get in trouble."
3. Your daughter complains that her younger sister pushes her buttons—with teasing and physical aggression—and then when she retaliates, she gets in trouble.
4. Both of your school-age children agree that an 8 PM bedtime in the middle of summer—when the sun does not go down until 9 PM and kids are always outside playing until then—is unrealistic and unfair.

Listen to your children. Validate their legitimate complaints and concerns. If you can change specific rules without compromising the Four Expectations, do it.

Finally, offer your children the right to request a meeting time to discuss specific requests or complaints about the Expectations or Rewards. This can either be a formal sit-down meeting involving the entire family or a one-on-one dialogue with one parent. Let the children know that you wish to be flexible and that their efforts to meet the Four Expectations will make it easier for you as parents to be flexible with rules and guidelines.

Chapter 8
"You're Grounded...Forever!" (And Other Appropriate Consequences)

In spite of the seven thousand books of expert advice, the right way to discipline a child is still a mystery to most fathers and...mothers. Only your grandmother and Ghengis Khan know how to do it.

~Billy Cosby

Sing out loud in the car even, or especially, if it embarrasses your children.

~Marilyn Penland

A Dirty Word

Consequences. What an awful sounding word. Does anyone ever hear, "Oh, those are lovely consequences!" It always seems to have a negative flavor, doesn't it? The truth is that consequence simply refers to what happens after something else.[20] The consequence of tapping an egg on the bowl is that the egg will crack. The consequence of a waiter giving good service is usually a good tip. I want you to get rid of your distaste for the term consequence, because *all* of your child's behaviors have consequences. Consequences are the most important tools in your toolbox that you use to shape your child's behavior.

The question is what types of consequences—and what specific consequences—tend to change behaviors quickly, safely, and permanently? Remember, we don't want to kill an ant with a sledgehammer.

We'll start with appropriate consequences for young children (about three to about nine years old).

100 Ways to Do Time Out (97 of Them Stink)

"Go to Time Out!" You've heard of Time Out. It's all the rage for parents who want to discipline some other way than beating the snot out of their kid. When I was a youngster, Time Out meant sitting in a corner with my nose against the wall. Not only did it seem to help curb whatever heinous sin I was committing that day, but it also cultivated my unparalleled expertise in differentiating paint scents.

If you read parenting books or watch any shows that advocate Time Out, you are aware that there are about 100 ways to do it. Most of them have serious flaws.

So what is the right way to do Time Out? Is there some magic to Time Out that represents the necessary and sufficient kernel? Is it really one minute for every year old? Will your six-year-old devolve to a Unabomber copycat if you only do four minutes? Can we do without some parts of Time Out to achieve the ultimate goal of changing behavior?

Let's start with some fundamentals. Time Out is not designed to be a punishment. Huh? Kids hate Time Out; doesn't that make it a

---

20 The Latin roots of the word *consequence* means "that which follows closely."

punishment? Well, yes and no. Punishment, by definition, involves any stimulus that reduces the frequency of a behavior. If Time Out works to reduce a behavior, then it indeed counts as a punishment.

But more importantly, Time Out acts as *reinforcement removal.* This isn't just a fancy-pants shrink term. It simply refers to the fact that some of the things parents do inadvertently reward or reinforce the very behaviors they want to get rid of. Time Out simply removes the child from that reinforcement or reward.

Yelling, screaming, nagging, threatening, reminding, mocking, and teasing are some of the chief culprits. What parent hasn't fantasized that if they only give their command louder or with a more serious tone that Junior will listen? However, your child isn't deaf and he isn't stupid. He's just busy soaking up the attention. Yes, believe it or not, the angry yelling, reminding and lecturing you hope will make a difference are in fact highly reinforcing to your child, because one of the primary things your child craves is your *attention.*

If we had to rate your child's response to your attention, POSITIVE ATTENTION would be a perfect 10 and NO ATTENTION would be a 0. What is surprising is that NEGATIVE ATTENTION would be a 7 or 8! Not a bad booby prize, huh?

The goal of Time Out is to temporarily withhold the reinforcing attention from the child, because it's just not a good idea to reinforce bad behavior. So how should Time Out actually be done? The essential elements of the following Time Out procedure were developed by clinical psychologist David Stein, Ph.D., author of *Ritalin is NOT the Answer.*

- First, find a really boring spot in the house. Remember, Time Out should offer as little interest and reinforcement as possible. Sitting on the bed with lots to look at and play with is NOT a good place for time out. A stool or boring chair in a quiet hallway is more like it.
- Do not give your child any warnings or count "1-2-3" before sending him to Time Out. Doing so only contributes to cognitive and behavioral dependence. It tells him, "I don't have to behave now; I'll move when she really means business." This prolonged interaction reinforces the problem behavior. Remember, any talking with your child is a form of attention

and is reinforcing. Why reinforce them twice before making them behave? Forget the "1-2-3 Method;" Parents in Charge use the "1 Method."

- Do not remind your child of what the rules and expectations are before a Time Out. It is *his* job to remember. Your kid is smart. Treat him like he is. You are going to go over the rules with your children at least twice during your Family Constitution meetings. After this, *they* are responsible to remember the rules. Of course, if they want a written list, that's up to them.

- Do not wait until Junior completes a problem behavior or repeats it several times. Intervene with Time Out at the mere hint of misbehavior; this will help increase his vigilance and help him think before he acts. This actually fosters the development of the frontal lobes, which are responsible for planning, organizing, and thinking ahead!

- Do not bargain or back down once you decide on a Time Out. Doing so teaches your child to obey only when you "mean business."

- Don't talk to Junior on the way to Time Out. Any discussion or argument reinforces the problem behavior. Just say, "Go to Time Out."

- Require immediate compliance with going to Time Out. <u>You are in charge</u>. (I'll discuss what to do if Junior does not go to Time Out later in Chapter 10.)

- Time Outs should be *about* one minute per year old— according to the adult's watch, not his. Don't fret too much about the exact length of Time Out; there is nothing scientific about doing one minute per year old. The point is removing Junior from the reinforcing situation for long enough that he thinks about what he did wrong and what rule was broken and then to conceive of what to do differently when the Time Out is complete. It's OK if your eight-year-old has a five-minute Time Out.

- There will be no talking, singing, playing, humming, bouncing, or bathroom requests allowed during Time Out. You will wait for perfect behavior for the right number of minutes. If he chooses to waste an hour or two while settling into perfect Time Out behavior, so be it. *No* reminders of proper Time Out behavior. This is very important.

- "Keester Rule": the butt stays on the chair! Too much moving around can be a child's way of self-reinforcing or self-reward. Don't allow it.
- After Time Out, insist that Junior tell you what he did wrong. This necessitates his active vigilance, awareness, and memory, a primary goal for working with a misbehaving child. If he can't remember or gives the wrong answer, it's back to Time Out for another round.
- Make certain he not only tells you the specific behaviors he did wrong, but which principle or rule he violated.[21] Hint: it always involves one of the Four Expectations.
- If Junior misbehaves on the way to Time Out, send him back to Time Out after the original Time Out is complete. Say, "Now I want you to remember how you behaved on the way to Time Out. Go back to Time Out." You are the boss, and you must not permit any misbehaving or testing behaviors.
- Require him to perform the correct behavior after he's told you what he did wrong. Establish yourself as the Parent in Charge.

Remember to reinforce him immediately when he begins complying with the original request or expectation. This gives you the chance to reinforce Junior positively by showering him with the attention he craves! Be as vigilant with positive and compliant behavior as you are with misbehavior. You want him to thrive on positive interaction and social reinforcement.

That's the scoop on the best way to do Time Out.

What to Do When You Are Not Home

OK, so Time Out makes sense at home. What about at the grocery store, park, or church? Where should the Time Out be completed at grandparents' house?

---

21 Consider this "benevolent brainwashing."

Most importantly, *do not* begin using Time Out elsewhere until you have established sound Time Out procedures at home and you have achieved significant success with it. Just like a teenager begins driving practice in a safe parking lot and then moves to the side streets and finally highways, you must solidify Time Out at home until you feel confident that it is working properly. Then you can transfer and generalize the process.

Once this occurs, you will feel more confident bringing your child out in public. Parks, churches, other children's homes, and school functions will likely have a relatively convenient location for Time Out. Try to find the most secluded or private spot; placing your child in a conspicuous place will embarrass him and make Time Out more of a punishment and will make it difficult to concentrate. As soon as you get to a new place, locate that spot. If Junior needs a Time Out, simply say, "Go to Time Out right there." Point to the spot. Say nothing else. Follow the rest of the Time Out procedure as you would at home.

The grocery store and other public places without a quality Time Out spot create a particular challenge. Since you can't sit your child in the produce freezer[22], you'll have to find a couple alternatives to regular Time Out. For public places like this, the first alternative is the "Silent Time Out." This requires Junior to remain silent for the length of Time Out. Understand that this will not work if you have not already established Time Out at home, so don't even bother if you haven't.

The second alternative involves delaying Time Out until you get home. While this is less effective than more immediately consequences, sometimes the specter of Time Out at home is enough to induce the child to rein in his own behavior. If Junior misbehaves, simply hold up one finger to indicate that he will have one Time Out when he gets home. If he misbehaves again, hold up two fingers; and so on. As soon as you get home, follow through with the number of Time Outs that Junior earned. Do not allow good behavior on the way home reduce the number or length of Time Outs; this will only encourage your child to butter you up to reduce consequences.

---

22 Although you'd have to admit it would be tempting.

What About the Supernanny?

A number of parents have asked me about the Supernanny method of Time Out. I have seen her program and I appreciate a great deal of the changes she brings to families. For example, she seems to support the notion that parents should be in charge. She also encourages unity between the parents regarding discipline. However, I perceive some fundamental flaws in the way she teaches Time Out.

First, she advocates physically placing the child in Time Out. Wrong! Except for infants and very young toddlers, Parents in Charge never force their child into Time Out. The child must go on his or her own. Carrying Junior or physically shepherding him to Time Out strongly reinforces the child; physical and verbal attention are both highly reinforcing. Not only does this intense attention reinforce the misbehavior that led to Time Out, but it encourages the child's belief that he can't do what he is told on his own. Essentially, the child believes that "Mom and Dad have to make me." This fundamentally flawed belief will undermine your child's sense of self-control. It also welcomes a physical battle and opens the possibility for injury to your child or yourself.

Second, she teaches parents to inform their child—even in the midst of a temper tantrum—what the child did to get the Time Out. This encourages cognitive dependence—the child doesn't have to think about what he did, because Mom and Dad are telling him. Remember, the main goal of Time Out is to get the child to think about his own behavior as it occurs or before. The child develops a "radar" of sorts, encouraging thoughts like "OK, what do I need to be doing right now? What rules am I tempted to break and what will be the consequence? What would be the best choice here?"

Principles/Limits of Consequences

As the Parent(s) in Charge, you are free to determine which consequences are most effective for your child. The best consequences are borne from sensible principles and are within reasonable limits. The following principles and limits can help parents decide which might be most helpful and appropriate.

Recently, a mother in New York made the news when she kicked her 10 and 12-year-old daughters out of the car for bickering. Even though the mother drove around the block and came back for the girls, she was later arrested for child endangerment, partly because by the time she had come back, the two girls had been separated. The younger girl was found relatively quickly, but there was a great outcry about the mother's discipline technique.

As you can tell, I'm all for tough discipline, including significant consequences. However, this choice was debatably excessive. A few principles for consequences will help those creative parents who want to be tough but would rather not end up on the evening news.

Most importantly, consequences must be **Reasonably Safe**. I confess, this is not rocket science. Some consequences such as kicking your kids out of the car are debatable. What if your children don't respond to your verbal admonitions and warnings? What if you are three miles from home? What if it is raining and the kids are not dressed appropriately? How old is old enough to walk home? What if you are in a notoriously bad neighborhood? What if you are on a very busy street? What if a child predator lives nearby?

One can see that the presumption of safety dwindles with each question. This is not a black-and-white issue. Some children are old and capable enough; an 8-year old, however, should not walk two miles home. Some streets and neighborhoods are safe enough, while highways and streets where the local sex perpetrator lurks are not. Some days are pleasant enough; sending your child out into a thunderstorm with no raincoat might not be the best idea. Each parent must decide whether the combined situation, environment, and child are sufficiently safe.

Consequences must be **Administered with Self-Control**. Consequences made in the heat of the moment or out of rage do not serve you or your child well. "That's it! Everyone is grounded for the rest of their lives!" might sound good when you have had it up to your neck with ridiculous, out-of-control behavior. I've been there, believe me. Children can sense when you are being impulsive, rather than measured. They perceive when you are out of control and making decisions emotionally, rather than rationally. This scares them—and not in a good way. Parents who make decisions emotionally lose their authority, rather than gain it. Instead of doling out consequences when you are enraged, take a few deep breaths, think it through, and *then* come up a consequence. I'm sure it will be brilliant.

Parents in Charge enforce consequences made in **Agreement with Both Parents**. Once, after my daughter disobeyed me by picking all of the tulips in our garden without permission, I came up with the brilliant idea to ground her from the yearly Mommy-Daughter dance later that week. As you can imagine (and I should have imagined), my wife did not appreciate this, especially after she had bought the ticket, secured a babysitter, and bought a dress. She had to use her executive veto power and cancel the punishment. The validity of my authority took a hit that day, as it should have. I did, however, snag my daughter's iPod for the week.

Removing Privileges

As I mentioned, Time Out works wonders for younger children. By the time children are eight or nine, privileges become more rewarding than attention, so Time Out becomes less effective. Because older children also possess a greater memory capacity, they can begin connecting behavior to consequences that occur further into the future.

For children eight and older, removing privileges such as toys, TV, video games, play dates[23], or dessert can effectively curb certain behaviors. The necessary component of this consequence is removing a privilege that is reinforcing enough to the child to make an impact. Because children have so many reinforcements in their lives, taking away just one might not have much of an impact. The child can simply find reinforcement elsewhere.

For example, if I attend a dinner buffet, I would not be fazed if someone removed the lasagna while leaving six or seven alternative entrees. I would be happy to settle for Beef Wellington or Chicken Vesuvio. If lasagna is by far my favorite entrée, however, and the only other choice was coconut-encrusted tilapia, I would be distraught[24]. Your child's collection of toys and privileges mirrors a buffet. Most children have several reinforcing activities and privileges from which to choose. To make a significant impact, either remove all of the options

---

23 When I become king, the term "play date" will be abolished—and whoever made it up will get 30 lashes with my son's wet pull-up.

24 Because coconut is evil. Scientific studies have conclusively proven this.

for a certain length of time or just remove the most reinforcing ones. Don't mess around.

Nonetheless, Parents in Charge are cautious not to remove once-in-a-lifetime privileges unless there has been a serious infraction of the Four Expectations. For example, if your child is set to play in a Little League championship game but received a D on a test that week, removing that privilege would be too heavy-handed. Instead, remove all electronics (TV, movies, video games, computer, cell phone, iPod) for a day or a week, depending on the age of the child and the seriousness of the misbehavior.

Remember, do not try this with younger children. Four-year-old girls are not capable of learning much from having their Polly Pockets taken away; similarly, your three-year-old isn't going to think deeply about his poor choices because he doesn't have his light saber for a day.

Teenagers

Just as it would be foolish to ground an 18-month old, Time Outs would be silly to use with your teenager. Young children are attention hogs (attention is by far the most reinforcing thing in their lives), but teenagers are not so moved by (or desirous of) your attention. By adolescence, freedoms and privileges become their primary reward. Parents in Charge intervene primarily in this sphere of reinforcement.

Because teenagers are gearing up for adulthood, they require a unique brand of parenting. Parents should seek every opportunity to parent them from an adult-adult framework. Taking away privileges when your teen breaks rules tends to foster a more adversarial, parent-child relationship. Your teen will likely chafe at this. Parents in Charge cultivate mutual respect by aiming for a more adult-adult relationship.

One way to achieve this is to conceive of all privileges as a form of payment that your teenager must earn on a week-to-week basis. As explained in the previous chapter, set the expectations your teen must follow. Be as specific as you can. Then enumerate which privileges may be earned by meeting those expectations. Stress that these are privileges, not rights. Then make clear that your teen will not get "paid" if she does not meet the Four Expectations. All privileges must now be earned.

111

The most powerful and reinforcing privileges for teenagers tend to be:

1. **Money**

Your teenager needs money to play, go out to movies, put gas in the car, cover her portion of car insurance, ride the bus, buy snacks, and numerous other activities that she greatly desires. Withhold allowance[25] when your teen fails to meet the Four Expectations. Fine your teen to reduce bad behavior patterns. This combination can be highly effective.

One single father I counseled had a son with a habit of cursing at home.[26] He began fining his son a dollar every time he cursed. Having depleted his entire paycheck after two days, he was unable to pay for a cafeteria lunch at school and had to pack his own lunch. After two weeks without any money to go out, the son decided to try a new vocabulary at home.

If your teenager has a job or receives a sum of money for birthdays or holidays, you have a legal right to control all of these monies. This is true until your child turns 18. Do not let the fact that your teen has a job to minimize your sovereignty. Do not allow your teen to work a part-time job if his behavior does not warrant it.

2. **Car**

This refers not only to having access to a car, but to a driver's license, permission to use the car, and access to car insurance. All of these should be available to your teenager only when he has earned it. You must avoid the temptation of needing your teen behind the wheel more than he needs it, or your advantage as a Parent in Charge will be severely compromised.

---

25 Your adolescent should not receive "allowance". Because your teen must earn his money, it makes more sense to call the money you give him a "paycheck". This reflects the real world, where one must earn a paycheck to pay for enjoyable activities and special things.

26 If you are guilty of modeling this pattern of behavior for your child, then you have no right to hold him accountable for it. First, stop your own cursing; then you can hold your child to that standard.

3. Electronics (i.e., computer, TV, video games, cell phone, iPod)

As I've said before, your teenager does not *need* electronic devices. She does not need a computer, internet access, a cell phone, or an iPod. People survived for many generations without these conveniences. I understand that many school assignments require internet access and word processing. That is what libraries, friends, and waking up early on a school day to use the school's computer are for.

4. Going out with friends

Your teen does not need to go out with friends. Your teen *wants* to go out with friends. Make going out with friends part of the weekly paycheck and your teen's motivation to meet the Four Expectations will skyrocket.

5. Grounding

Grounding has always been a popular punishment/reinforcement removal technique. Although it can be used effectively, it can also be overused. Some parents ground their teens for everything, including a bad test grade, coming home late, back-talk, failing to do chores adequately, and on and on. This constant flow of punishment is dangerous because a child under constant punishment can easily feel defeated. A defeated child is an unmotivated child. An unmotivated child does not strive to meet the Four Expectations, which is the exact opposite of what you want!

If you ground your older child or teenager, make sure the grounding is more of a punishment for the child than it is for you. If grounding forces you into the role of prison warden, then it is likely to be rewarding for your teen; they can sense when you are miserable. Make sure that all reinforcers in the home are unavailable, such as movies, TV, video games, computer, cell phone; otherwise, your teen will hunker down to a nice long electronic vacation.

Chapter 9

How to Win the *"Worst Parent of the Year"* Award

It behooves a father to be blameless if he expects his child to be.

~Homer

Don't worry that children never listen to you;
worry that they are always watching you.

~Robert Fulghum

Jason

Jason was a twelve-year-old spark plug who was in full puberty and was every bit the adolescent. Although I describe him as a "spark plug", his parents' description of him was not as kind. He definitely fit the criteria for OD: *Obnoxious Disorder, Severe Type*. When I met Jason, he was one of the most vile, rude, entitled little monsters with whom I have ever worked. I remember purposely scheduling him before a lunch break or right before going home, because I needed a break after sitting with him for 45 minutes. It was exhausting and often exasperating work.

When I began working with his parents on reestablishing a proper family hierarchy, I was convinced that if they did the right things, their son would soon become a more respectful, considerate, law-abiding family citizen. A few weeks into our work together, not only were things worse (as they often become for a short time), but they were *terrible*. Conflicts devolved into fights; fights snowballed into World Wrestling Federation matches. The family had even become intimately acquainted with the local police. My method was not working.

One of the mistakes I made with the family was failing to more fully investigate how the parents were functioning. I only looked at how they responded to Jason's inappropriate behavior and attitude. On the surface, they both appeared to believe in clear limits, consistent consequences, and a united parental front.

During one of our more hopeless appointments, Jason sat in my office with a look that blended boredom and hostility. His mother eagerly recounted her son's weekly sins; she seemed relieved, as if she were going to confession for him. After she described an incident where Jason cursed at his father, Jason mumbled under his breath (but loud and clear enough for us both to hear), "I do it and I'm the Devil; Dad does it and it's no big deal." In a moment of humility and compassion, his mother turned to me and said, "My husband certainly has cursed him out a lot; I sometimes can't blame Jason for fighting back." That certainly piqued my curiosity.

Over time, I learned a bit about Jason's father—a 20-year veteran of the police department. Not only was he a heavy drinker with a short and nasty temper, but he had hardly been involved in Jason's life as a youngster. The mother told me about several instances where his decision-making had become severely impaired. During one drinking binge, he urinated on Jason's bed while he was sleeping; another time he called Jason's principal and shamed Jason right in front of him, calling him extremely derogatory names that would make any spell check blush.

Yet another time, he pinned Jason on the floor in front of one of his friends, rubbing his face in the carpet and claiming that "Skateboarding is for pussies; if you learned how to wrestle you would know what to do right now." He was also critical of Jason's interests, which did not include traditional sports like football and baseball—sports in which he himself had excelled in high school. Instead, he mocked Jason's interest in skateboarding and Manga (the Japanese comic-book art form).

Because I never want to presume that one parent's word about another parent is completely accurate, I invited Jason's father to one of our family sessions. I inquired about his drinking; he emphatically denied having any problem with alcohol. However, he did admit to most of the things he had said to Jason. He weakly justified them, suggesting that his parenting style would "man him up more than his mother does."

It didn't take long before I concluded that if this man were my father, I wouldn't respect him any more than Jason did. I couldn't justify Jason's blatant disrespect toward his parents, nor could I support his chronic rule-breaking. But I now could empathize with the boy and his mother, who was desperately trying to establish some kind of union in her family. It had become clear to me that the union's disarray did not begin with Jason, but with the marriage. This was not a unit of authority that inspired love or respect.

Remember, just because parents should be in control in theory does not mean that all parents are equally deserving of their children's respect. The ideal, as described earlier, includes two parents who earn their child's respect through genuine love and firm but fair discipline. However, some parents either take their role to one extreme (the *Captain von Trapp* or *Great Santini* style of parenting) or do things that invalidate their position in the family.

Passive, Authoritative, and Authoritarian Parenting

Mental health professionals describe a range of parenting styles from passive to authoritarian.

	Extreme------Moderate/Healthy/Valid------Extreme		
Classic Term	Passive	Authoritative	Authoritarian
Modern Term	Passive Parent	Parent in Charge	Drill Instructor
Theme	"Anything Goes"	Parents First	Tyranny
Children's Place in the Family Hierarchy	First	Second	None

The first extreme style is *Passive Parenting* (otherwise known as Submissive or Wimpy Parenting). Passive parenting refers to a family hierarchy that places children first. These parents tend to be hyper-committed to their children, allowing the bulk of their lives to revolve around their precious cherubs. They even prioritize (purposely or inadvertently) their children above their spouse. Instead of date night with a spouse or boyfriend/girlfriend, the passive parent sacrifices all of their time to entertain and be with their child. Furthermore, when conflicts arise between child and parent, the passive parent tends to empathize more easily with the child.

The hallmark of the passive parent is a general permissive attitude toward behavior. While they do not necessarily approve of all behaviors, they do not seem to intervene, either because they do not desire to control their children or because they do not know how to alter their behavior. Passive parents maintain a slight fear of their children; they tend to avoid their children's judgment or anger at all costs.

On the opposite end of the spectrum is the *Authoritarian*. The Authoritarian (or *Drill Instructor*) does not believe in choices. My child either obeys or suffers. My child does not need my affection; it only needs to obey, because I know best. Period. The Authoritarian does not believe in positive reinforcement. Punishment is the primary tool; fear is the primary motivator.

The *Authoritative Parent* (what I call a *Parent in Charge*) believes that love and discipline are two sides of the same coin. Because I love my child, I discipline her. Because I discipline my child, there is more room to show love and affection and all of that wonderful warm fuzzy stuff.

Things That Invalidate Parental Authority:

Drug use/abuse

Obviously, a father who shoots up heroin and robs convenience stores to fund his habit cannot engender much respect from his child. A mother who regularly smokes marijuana would have a hard time earning respect from other adults, law enforcement, and teachers. As if that weren't enough, how can the parent who abuses drugs expect a child to "say 'no' to drugs?"

Excessive alcohol use, binge drinking

Responsible, moderate drinking does not invalidate a parent. In fact, it can model self-control and respect for the rule of law. On the other hand, driving under the influence (even mildly under the influence), buying alcohol for minors, frequently getting drunk and doing foolish things, and getting drunk in the presence of children are all unacceptable. A reasonable child will rightly perceive that parent as a buffoon, rather than someone they should respect and obey.

Physical abuse

This one should be obvious. Some parents mistakenly use physical intimidation and aggression in order to force respect, believing that their children need to be frightened into obeying and respecting them. Unfortunately, abusive parents tend to unwittingly build resentment, lack of respect, hatred, and anxiety, as well as a pattern of abusing others. Parents in Charge know how to reserve the use of intimidation and force for only the gravest circumstances.

Frequently losing one's temper/becoming overly aggressive

I have three children. I know how angry children can make a parent. I understand the intensity of emotion that can overwhelm a parent when a child is rude, disrespectful, and even in your face with it. However, parents must maintain their composure; losing one's cool during conflicts really does teach children to do the same.[27] I'm not talking about the occasion outburst. You needn't worry about the child who hears "You guys drive me insane!" every once in a while.

Emotional abuse

Name-calling, picking on, put-downs, unwelcome teasing, humiliation, and mocking your child communicates an utter lack of respect. The only logical response is to respond in kind by denying respect to the parent. Teenagers in particular will seek vengeance in any way they can, including blatant defiance, breaking rules, and speaking ill of the emotionally abusing parent. Who can blame them?

Threatening child, sibling, or other parent with physical harm or drastic punishment

Fear does not breed respect or self-control. While I am not advocating the idea of *karma*, it doesn't take a rocket scientist to know that respect and self-control breed further respect and self-control.

But is it inappropriate or excessive to threaten your child with punishment? As with any form of discipline, it is indeed appropriate and even necessary to tell your children what consequences will materialize if your child misbehaves. If you conceive and express it in a thoughtful, self-controlled, measured way, this constitutes a warning. Doing so impulsively or out of rage is more of a threat.

Not allowing the child sufficient freedom for his/her develop- mental needs

Withstanding the temptation to keep your child in a cage or on a leash is not enough (although a must).[28] It is essential that you reward your child's developmental maturation with increased trust, freedom, and privileges. While most overprotective parents are motivated by love, when their limits become too restrictive, the result is often rebellion.

---

27 Controlled, measured spanking with younger children does not model aggres-sion or violence as a solution to conflict. See Chapter 10.

28 Unless your teenage daughter wants to date, in which case keeping her in a cage until she turns 25 or so is highly recommended.

Children must have freedom to explore relationships places while they still have the benefit of parental guidance and protection.

I have seen far too many 18-year-olds with overly restrictive parents who leave home for college and end up going berserk from the deluge of newly found freedom. Adolescents need a slow, steady introduction to adult-like freedoms, or they will not know how to handle them when the shackles of restrictive parenting are removed.

Poor Modeling

Parents who rely on the "Do as I say, not as I do" philosophy ignore decades of research and millennia of common sense about child development. A parent's actions are far more instructive than his or her words. If you swear up a storm but expect your child to control his tongue, you are in for a "colorful" surprise. Similarly, if you eat Twinkies and Doritos for dinner but try to make your seventh grader eat broccoli and brown rice, you will damage your alliance with your child. Children are keenly aware of injustice; they are not easily fooled by the idea that parents should not be held to the same standards as children. Rather, children know that parents should in fact be held to a *higher* standard than they are.

I'm all for common-sense rebellion. If your child's school is trying to force your daughter to recite a prayer to Allah and you are a Christian family, go ahead and encourage your child to defy the teachers and school. If your son's coach offers him steroids, support your child's refusal. On the other hand, supporting a general sense of defiance toward adult authority is counterproductive at best and ridiculous at worst.

In one psychiatric hospital where I worked, we had to check all items that parents brought to their children during visitation. Without fail, there was always one parent who tried to sneak their child some contraband, such as food, cell phones, or drugs. One father tried to sneak his child some Ritalin because he was convinced the doctors weren't paying proper attention to his son's ADHD symptoms!

Here is the message this sent: rules don't really need to be followed. We brought you to this place for help, but we do not trust that their rules, boundaries, and limits are appropriate. I know that we insist you follow rules at home, but it is acceptable to subvert them here. I am your ally in doing so.

It is shocking how many parents are damaging their children and marriages by acting as allies in encouraging rebellion, often without the other parent knowing. This wrecks both parents' authority.

Excessive Conflict/Disrespect Between Parents

Remember, children learn to do what they see, not what they are told. If you and your spouse are verbally, emotionally, or physically abusive to each other, you cannot expect to tell your children that they must respect both of you. Why should they? If Dad yells at Mom, berates her, ignores her, mocks her, you should expect that your children will do the same. Some parents take out their subconscious anger toward their spouse by seeking revenge against the other parent by allowing their child to misuse or abuse that other parent. This is simply unacceptable.

Take a good hard look at your parenting. Do you do anything to invalidate your authority? Do you do anything to invalidate the authority of your spouse or any other important adult in your child's life? If you do, understand that change must first happen within; then you can shift your attention to changing your child.

Chapter 10

To Spank or Not to Spank (And Other Modern Parenting Challenges)

Never raise your hand to your kids. It leaves your groin unprotected.

~Red Buttons

And though you may compel a child with blows, what are you to do with him when he is a young man no longer amenable to such threats and confronted with tasks of far greater difficulty?

~Quintillian (circa 35-95 AD)

Spanking

Bring up the topic of spanking and you will quickly see that many parents feel very strongly about the subject. There are passionate, rational advocates on either side of the issue. Some states have movements afoot to ban spanking altogether and even criminalize spanking children.[29] Because of the cultural shift away from spanking, many parents are afraid to spank their children out of fear that others will perceive them as abusive or that the Department of Child Services will take their children away.

On the other side are some "pro-spanking" advocates who are frankly more than a bit creepy. They almost gleefully extol the virtues of spanking their children, almost as if it were a rite of passage or a necessary part of their daily diet. "Spank early, spank often" reflects their motto. Pro-spankers use spanking as the primary tool of discipline, often to shame their children and control the minutest details of the child's life. This twisted mentality and practice certainly *is* abusive; it should be relegated to the garbage dump.

My professional and person opinion on spanking is a moderate one: while some children react poorly to spanking, some children can be disciplined quite effectively and safely with spanking. It all depends on how and when parents administer the spanking.

One of the arguments against spanking begins with the acknowledgement that some parents misuse spanking. I absolutely agree with those who believe that using spanking incorrectly can do long-term damage to a child's psyche. However, getting rid of spanking because some parents abuse it is like getting rid of cooking because some chefs overcook food. Let's not throw the baby out with the bathwater.

I have spanked each of my three children. It is not something I am proud of, nor is it something I am ashamed of. I spank for two reasons and *only* two reasons. First, I spanked in response to an extremely dangerous behavior, such as jumping out into the street (eldest daughter) or throwing a rock at a moving car (my son). I used the spanking as a shock. Second, I spanked my child for not going immediately to Time Out when commanded. Each of my kids tried this once; they thought

---

29 Parents can still spank each other all they like, but that's a topic for another book.

they could just leave Time Out or outright refuse it. Three swats on the butt convinced them otherwise. Since then, Time Out has worked like a charm for each of them; I have not needed to spank them again.

Spanking is a form of punishment. Punishment by definition is any stimulus that decreases the frequency of a behavior. If spanking your child after he picks his nose at the table gets him to stop, it has served as a punishment. If, however, it does not work—if the nose-picking increases or stays the same—then spanking was not really a punishment. Rather, it was a reinforcement.

The key to understanding punishment hinges on two facts. First, while punishment can often reduce the frequency of a behavior, its effects are usually short-term. Second and more importantly, punishment can never teach a new, more desirable behavior. Punishment will never be effective for teaching your child how to set the table properly. Positive reinforcement is far more effective in teaching and increasing desirable behaviors.

I am not saying that parents need to spank their children. But remember what spanking does for the child: it sends a message that there are certain lines that must not be crossed. If your child crosses that more significant line, there will be a swift, serious, and painful consequence.

To conclude, spanking can indeed be abusive, but it is *not* abusive if done properly. Here are the keys to effective, humane spanking:

- Spanking should never be done out of rage. If you are losing your temper, don't spank. If you cannot spank without being calm, don't spank. Remember, the actual spanking is not what can damage the child; rather, it is the rage associated with it.
- Spanking must only be done on the butt. Not the face, head, arm, back, legs, or anywhere else. This is to protect your child from injury and unnecessary shame, which are both clearly counterproductive to discipline.
- A parent should always explain the reason for the spanking before spanking: "Mommy is going to have to spank you, because you did not go to Time Out like you were told." This exhibits self-control to the child and makes it clear why it is happening.

- If you spank and your child laughs at you or does not respond by submissively, you are either not spanking hard enough or there is a fundamental relationship problem that makes your child resistant to the pain of spanking.
- Spanking should cease by age six or seven. Any form of physical punishment should not be used with older children.

Technology

Every generation of parents has to cope with next generation's set of interests. Elvis gave parents fits in the 1950's. In the 60's, hippies drove parents insane. Today's parents face enormous, unique challenges that come from the constantly advancing technology, making it almost impossible for parents to keep up.

The first major challenge is the nearly ubiquitous cell phone. Most teenagers have cell phones these days, as do many grade school children. Parents appreciate the freedom it gives their children to contact them from almost anywhere; they also use the cell phone as a way of checking in with their child. The cell phone is indeed a wonderful invention.

Of course, it comes with a host of temptations and difficulties. First, because parents often want their children to have and use their cell phone, it no longer appears as a privilege to the child. The child begins to believe that the phone and use of the phone is a right— almost a necessary part of life—so that having to earn it makes little sense to them.

Second, cell phones are incredibly difficult for parents to monitor. Whereas land lines are generally limited to certain rooms in the house, cell phones can be kept under pillows, under the covers, and in backpacks, so that parents have little idea that their child is using their phone, especially late at night. I have worked with many families where teens and even pre-teens have been receiving and responding to text messages until the wee hours of the morning.[30] The same is true for cell phone calls.

Recall the children in William Golding's *Lord of the Flies*. These children were stranded on a deserted island with no adults to care for or provide limits for them; nor did they have anyone acting as a moral and ethical authority or model. With no authoritative boundaries imposed

---

30 Remember, a sleep-deprived child is a dysfunctional child.

on them, their society quickly devolved and disintegrated. Their primitive, baser instincts took control; chaos ensued, bringing death and ruin. Now, imagine if the adults (parents and teachers) had been there. Presuming they were able and reasonably moral people, there would have been far less chaos and destruction. The adults could have investigated the island, organized a reasonable and safe social order, and determined a wise course of self-discipline.

Today's children have been similarly stranded on an island of rapidly evolving technology and virtual socialization for which they have had no training. The adults who supposedly would train them are generally ignorant, unavailable, or unwilling to train them. For many adults, today's technology is foreign and frightening; other parents simply have little time to monitor their children's foray into the digital social world.

Many parents often have a perceived need for their children to use these technologies. Some believe that they must allow and even insist on cell phones in order to maintain communication with them; they feel safer being able to contact their child wherever they are. Sadly, many allow cell phone and private internet communication in order to avoid the ridicule of their already disparaging and pestering children.

How many children have been trained to deal with the trials and tribulations of society, especially the cyber society? Too few. How can we expect our children to be prepared for these things? They are simply too young, too immature. They do not yet own the requisite skills and emotional level-headedness to cope with the kind of drama that often stems from these technologies. As a result, we see children creating their own independent society, hidden from their parents. This "screen society"—played out on cell phones, Facebook, and instant messaging—can be quite intense and dramatic. We should not be surprised that children are likely to struggle in this alternative, hidden society.

What are the solutions?

First, children must be taught from an early age that cyber communication must only be used as a supplement for live, face-to-face relationships. Allowing younger children to begin and maintain relationships via texting, Facebook, and other online avenues creates a template for future relationships. Limiting these avenues when they get older then becomes far more difficult. Rather, parents must limit them to simple e-mails to relatives and pen-pals. MySpace and Facebook can wait.

Second, parents must insist from day one that they be privy to all electronic communication. That means children may not use cell phones, the internet, and any messaging programs unless the parent owns the password and can monitor any messages or content of any electronic communication at any time. The understanding is that the parent has the right to monitor these conversations *in order to maintain the child's safety*. The purpose of this openness is not to reduce the child's privacy to practically nothing; rather, the purpose is to assure both parent and child that the child will be monitored and protected from anything dangerous. That is, after all, the parent's primary goal. If the child finds this unacceptable, then the child should not receive the privilege until it becomes acceptable. For the Parent in Charge, this is a non-negotiable limit.

Third, parents must stop presuming that children need cell phones or that they need their child to have a cell phone. This is simply not the case. Yes, cell phones are a marvelously convenient technology; it is wonderful that parents can text or call their child for myriad reasons, including emergencies, managing rides, checking in and checking up, and giving reminders. I fully support adolescents earning the privilege of having a cell phone. However, almost every home, school, and public place still has a land line. It is not as if a child is marooned on a desert island if he does not have a cell phone with him. Not only is there a good chance that one of his peers has a cell phone your child can borrow or use, but if your child cannot get to a landline phone, then chances are he is somewhere he should not be.

Cell phones should be considered a privilege, like use of the internet, computer, or video games. A child can survive without a cell phone and you can survive without your child having a cell phone. In fact, when your child is temporarily without a cell phone, a wonderful opportunity arises for you to discuss alternative communication plans. This is always a good idea anyway, since many children like to use the "my cell's battery was out" or "I wasn't getting reception" excuse when they don't check in or receive a call from a parent. A child should always know how to find a land line or alternative method of contacting a parent.

Third, cell phones should be shut off or given to a parent in the evening, before bedtime. During the school week, there should be no communication via cell or internet after 8 PM for junior high students and 10 PM for high school students.[31] It is far too easy for adolescents to become entangled in late-night conversations that postpone bedtime. Remove the temptation for them until they prove mature enough to monitor themselves satisfactorily.

Video Games

The good old days of *Pong*, *Missile Command*, and *RBI Baseball* are long gone. Today's games are far more engaging—a veritable feast for the eyes and ears. Some of these games, however, are insanely violent and involve content so intense and outrageous that calling them "mature" or "adult" does injustice to both adjectives. It is hard to fathom how parents could possibly allow their children to play games like those in the *Grand Theft Auto* series. That some parents are this ignorant or permissive suggests that the devolution of our species is in full force.

There are violent games and then there are **violent games**. Games that simulate World War II battles often show blood, but these are not nearly as egregious as the simulation games that encourage immoral behavior, promote a perverse focus on death, or celebrate gratuitous violence. Any parent who allows these games in their home automatically invalidates their authority.

If you are a parent who allows these games in your home, stop reading this book immediately. Go into your family room or den, grab the games, and destroy them with a hammer. They are beyond useless; they are harmful to children. I am not going to join the debate over whether violent video games cause violent behavior. That question is debatable. What is not debatable is that these games offer nothing positive to your child—emotionally, academically, relationally, intellectually, or spiritually. Get rid of them.

What level of violence should be acceptable? There are essentially three types of violent video games; each has its own pros and cons:

---

31   For weeknights. While out on weekends, teens should keep their cell phone with them until they get home.

1. War games (*Call of Duty, Command & Conquer*)

These somewhat realistic strategy and shooter games involve blowing up tanks and shooting human enemy soldiers. Some involve significant, realistic blood and guts, but the violence is impersonal and relatively detached.

2. Alien/monster shooter games (*World of Warcraft, Halo, Lord of the Rings*)

These hugely popular games involve fantasy worlds and fictional scenarios. There is blood, but the game's focus is mostly positive, involving relatively wholesome goal-directed behavior (e.g., kill the evil monsters).

3. Realistic plot/assassin games (*Grand Theft Auto, NARC, Crime Life: Gang Wars*)

I lied; these games have no redeeming value whatsoever. They combine the worst of realistic, gratuitous human violence with glorification of an immoral, thuggish lifestyle. The violence is personal, intimate, and often freakish.

In my opinion, children should never play games from the last group. Teenagers should be allowed to play games from either of the first two, while pre-teens should not be playing any of these. Have them stick to sports, strategy, and education games until they are older.

Television

All of the televisions in your home are yours. You have a right and responsibility to control what your children view on television. Your children do not have a right to cable or to watch whatever programs they like. You set the limits for programming and the amount of TV your child watches.

As for what programming is acceptable, consider the following. First, children should not be allowed to watch MTV; that channel is worthless. Second, children should not watch any programs that the Parents in Charge have not already examined to determine their appropriateness. Third, there is nothing positive for children on reality television shows.[32]

If for some reason (perhaps a drunken stupor or before you elevated yourself to a Parent in Charge) you allowed your child to have a television in her room, get rid of it. Sell it on eBay. If I find out that you read this book and still allow your child to have a television in his room, I will find you and whack you over the head with my book. Get it out of there; children should not have their own television. It's ridiculous!

Dating

What to do when your child or adolescent wants to date? Should the parent be in charge there? You betcha. Why? Because what 13-year-old has the wisdom and experience to make solid and healthy decisions about dating? About sexual boundaries? About how to protect her heart? Very few. To assume that your kid is somehow above that or immune from the temptations, trials, and tribulations of dating is incredibly naïve.

Kids should not be dating until they are well into their teens. Yes, that is your decision as a parent. Your child does not have the *right* to date before then, no matter what their Freshman English teacher tells them about *Romeo and Juliet*.

What should you do when your child indicates or expresses romantic inclinations and desires? Listen. Understand. Empathize. Remember. Enjoy your child's passion, innocence, and wide-eyed expectations. Validate the normality and healthiness of age-appropriate desires and interests. Reinforce for your child that you cannot nor would you try to control his or her feelings or thoughts about the opposite sex. Yet, you must state your united expectations and boundaries regarding dating and sexual behavior. This is far easier if you began this process in early childhood and, conversely, exceedingly difficult if you try to start setting boundaries and establishing a proper hierarchy when this issue comes to the fore.

There is no one set of boundaries and limits regarding dating that works for all parents, cultures, and subcultures. However, I feel strongly

---

32 There is nothing positive for adults on most reality TV shows either, but we all have our guilty pleasures…

that parents can and should take an active role in their child's dating experience, especially in the beginning.

Dating Rules

1. You may go on one-on-one dates when you are 16.
2. You may go on group dates when you are 14, under the following conditions:
   - An adult whom we know and approve of chaperones
   - The chaperone will have reasonable supervision of the whole group
   - There is a prescribed activity or reasonable structure to the group date
3. You may not be alone and unsupervised with a peer of the opposite sex until you have exhibited significant maturity, insight, and an ability to establish and maintain appropriate boundaries with the opposite sex. This process can be established through a series of conversations with Mom or Dad. Until then, you may not be alone with an opposite sex peer in your room, the basement, the attic, or for a lengthy time in the car.
4. You may only date someone whom Mom and Dad have met personally and to whose parents we have spoken. We simply need to know what kind of values they espouse and what limits they have.
5. If your boyfriend or girlfriend proves disrespectful to you, our family, or our property, you will not be allowed to date that person.
6. You may date only while you follow these rules. Breaking these rules will result in significant, if not severe, restrictions on your freedom to date.

Divorced and Single Parents

A few years ago, I had a client who was a single mother of four children. One day she came to our session wearing a t-shirt with a "Superman" logo on it. I was touched by her self-respect; she clearly honored her role as mother and the enormity of the work she did to take care of her children.

I am often tempted to believe that all single parents are taking speed. I have no idea how they do it; I know I couldn't. It is hard enough to parent with an equally committed, equally able partner. Parenting without that benefit requires Herculean strength, patience, sacrifice, and tolerance.[33] Single and divorced parents often have a disadvantage in establishing themselves as a Parent in Charge. They must play the role of mother, father, doctor, tutor, emotional scratching post, chauffeur, good cop, bad cop, cook, maid, mentor, and every other role ideally shared by two able parents.

The greatest necessity for a divorced or single parent is establishing and maintaining a parenting partner or team of parenting partners. For the divorcee, the ex-spouse represents the ideal choice. This illustrates the need for divorcing parents to sacrifice their own personal vendettas and pain in order to commit to active co-parenting. Parents who forgo this essentially shoot themselves in the foot, hand, and shoulder.

Children of divorce desperately need parents who commit to unity in child rearing and training. Parents must perpetually unite in their expectations, limits, consequences, and rewards. Parents in Charge continually use phrases like, "Mom and Dad agree that…" and "Your Dad and I believe that…" Disunity between Mom and Dad will surely result in the diminished authority of either parent or both parents.[34]

Divorced co-parents can use *The Family Constitution* to achieve unity. It can help both parents coordinate expectations, limits, boundaries, and consequences. It can also acknowledge differences between parents and help parents determine how much flexibility is appropriate as children go from one parent to the other.

The single parent must look elsewhere for parenting partners. Grandparents, uncles, neighbors, coaches, scout leaders, and teachers are all appropriate potential partners. These partners need not be someone who spends a great deal of time with the child. Rather, these key people can offer their promotion of the single parent by validating that parent's authority, expressing reverence for the work of that parent, and on occasion, offering a gentle rebuke for not meeting the Four Expectations.

---

33 And a healthy diet consisting of plenty of coffee and vodka.
34 There is no medieval torture device brutal enough for the parent who purposely diminishes the authority of an ex-spouse out of revenge.

Dealing with Other Parents' Children

Now that you have become a Parent in Charge, you have established yourself as the authority of your household and set eminently reasonable expectations. You have become expert at motivating and disciplining your children. Your children are now more respectful and obedient; you are cheerfully amazed to learn how much more pleasant your interactions are with them. You can take them to the grocery store without fearing the worst. Although there are plenty of challenges and bumps, the house runs smoothly. Your family functions like the Roman Empire in all its glory.[35]

Like the Roman Empire, you will eventually have to deal with foreign invasions. Inevitably, other children—peers, cousins, stepchildren—will come to your home or will be present when you go elsewhere. Unless my ideas are universally incorporated and perfected by every family in the world[36], you will likely have to deal with a series of children and families who do not share your values, boundaries, limits, and expectations. You will bear the unenviable burden of interacting with other parents' children.

When other children enter your home, it is crucial that you perceive them as guests in *your* home. They are not wild animals who have free rein. They are entering your sovereign domain with your permission. They must follow the rules and expectations of your home.

When a new child comes to your home, sit the child and the parent down and explain all the rules. Enumerate the consequences for misbehavior. Have the child and parent sign a contract; tell them it is legally binding.

Of course, I'm joking. You don't need to explain the rules and expectations unless the child's behavior warrants an intervention. If another child in your home begins to misbehave, simply explain to the child:[37]

> "We have certain rules here. You must be safe, you must respect others with your body and your words; and you must obey me if I ask you to do something. I know that

---

35 Without the gladiators and temples, of course.
36 My Nobel Peace Prize acceptance speech is nearly complete.
37 After a while, you can have your child explain the rules to a child new to your home.

all children make a mistake or misbehave sometimes. If that happens, I will tell you to go to Time Out, which is on that chair right there. All you have to do is sit for five minutes. As long as you can follow that, you are welcome in my house."

Is it acceptable to give other children Time Out in your home? Of course! Briefly explain the Time Out procedure. If the child refuses Time Out, then you have a right and a responsibility to get the child out of your home immediately, either by calling the parents to pick him up or by taking the child home. Then explain your disciplinary procedure to the parents and inform them that their child is more than welcome in your home again if he can respect your rules and authority.

A few cautionary words about disciplining another parent's child:

1. Do not spank or use any other form of physical discipline with anyone else's child unless you have express permission from that parent to discipline that child exactly as you would yours. Some close friends and relatives might allow this, but presuming this puts you at great risk.

2. Remember that it is not your job to train another parent's child. Discipline for your child's friends should focus on maintaining the safety of the children and relative order in your home. Do not nit-pick or feel compelled to focus on the same behaviors you are training with your child.

3. Unless the children's safety or your Ming vases are at risk, let children work out their own conflicts. Monitor roughhousing, mean talk, and other difficulties between them, but try not to intervene unless one of them comes to you to referee. Children need to experience conflict without the presence of a referee. Feel free to talk about the incident later with your child; this provides the opportunity to teach your child how to resolve conflicts and examine whether your child should play with the other child.

4. Continue to discipline your child in the presence of other children, just as you would at home. The exception to this: make every effort to spank your child in private, not in front of the child's peer.

College-Age Children

So you finally saw your child off to college. Congratulations! You made it. Are you done parenting? Not quite. There are still plenty of opportunities for you to effect some positive change and influence on your young man or woman.

First, the list of rewards changes dramatically. You are no longer the gatekeeper of freedoms and privileges—except money. Hopefully, your young adult craves three things from you:

1. Your respect
2. Financial support, backing, and connections
3. Your wisdom and knowledge

Your influence is generally limited to these spheres.

The expectations you have for your young adult also changes. While your young adult navigates the academic and social challenges at school, you expect relatively safe behavior, respect, and reasonable success in school (essentially a return on your financial investment). As long as your young adult is not drinking himself into oblivion, is reasonably respectful to you during phone calls and visits, and is achieving grades appropriate to his ability, he is fulfilling his obligation to you.

It is entirely reasonable that when Junior returns to your home for summer that you present some reasonable expectations. First, you can expect that your young adult occupy him or herself to a responsible degree. Want to have an adolescent plopping herself on the couch, sleeping until 2 PM, and talking on the phone all evening? Me neither. It is reasonable to set an expectation that by a certain date, your young adult must occupy herself with one of three options:

- Full-time job
- Full-time summer school
- Half-time job and half-time school

If your son or daughter refuses to comply or makes only a feeble attempt at securing one or the other or both, then he or she should not be welcome in your home.

You can make an exception for the young adult whose academic performance is particularly strong or who clearly has put forth extraordinary effort during the school year. Such an adolescent deserves some flexibility in the expectation to work during vacations. Simply make the expectations clear.

Appendix A
The Family Constitution Worksheet

Preamble

We, the _____ Family, in order to form a more perfect family union, establish justice, insure peace in our home, provide for all our needs, promote the development of all family members, establish reasonable limits and boundaries, and teach godly principles and knowledge, do ordain and establish this Constitution for our family.

Section I: The Structure of our Family

The leaders and originators of this family are Mom and Dad. Their authority comes both from God and from common sense, as well as their knowledge, experience, and wisdom in caring for this family.

Both Mom and Dad are equal authorities in this family. Dad has final say in all matters, because there are times when one person will need to make a final decision about matters. However, Mom's say is equal to Dad's; when Dad is not present, all rules and expectations must be followed as if Dad were there. The same applies when Mom is not present. Furthermore, all respect given to one parent must also given to the other; any disrespect shown toward one parent will be seen as disrespect toward both parents.

Grandma and Grandpa occupy the position of authority in all matters when Mom and Dad are not present. The family rules fully apply; they have authority to enforce the rules.

When the children are by themselves downstairs or outside, none of them is in charge of the others. _____ (the eldest) is not the authority over his/her younger siblings. However, because he/she is older, he/she has more responsibility and can remind either sibling of the rules and possible consequences. It is not his/her job to discipline the others; in fact, he/she may not discipline the others.

Section II: The Four Expectations

All _____ children must adhere to the Four Expectations; almost all rules fall under these four categories. If they follow these expectations, they will not only earn Mom and Dad's respect, but will also earn trust, appropriate freedoms and privileges at an age-appropriate level.

The first and most important expectation in our family is to **BE SAFE**. This means ensuring your own safety, the safety of your family, and the safety of the home. Specifically, this means:

_____

_____

_____

_____

_____

_____

_____

_____

_____

_____

_____

_____

_____

The next expectation is **RESPECT**. This includes respect for all members of the household, starting with your elders. It also means respecting your coaches, teachers, pastors/priests/rabbis, the police, and all other respectable adults. Finally, it includes respect of all family property. Specifically, respect refers to:

_____

_____

_____

_____

_____

_____

_____

_____

_____

_____

_____

_____

Next, all children in this family are expected to **OBEY** the family rules. It also means that you are generally expected to do what you are told when you are told, without complaining, arguing, or dawdling.

Mom and Dad do not expect robotic obedience; you have important things to do and we know that sometimes it is impossible to do what you are told immediately. We are committed giving you grace and being patient when appropriate. You may ask for exceptions when you have a good reason, as long as you do so respectfully and are willing to comply.

Mom and Dad also recognize that there are times when you should not obey authorities. We will discuss these situations with you individually, but here are a few clear instances when we want you to disobey or refuse to comply:

_____

_____

_____

_____

_____

_____

_____

_____

_____

_____

_____

Finally, all family members are expected to do their fair share of **WORK**. Just as Mom and Dad work very hard at both a career and at home, our children are expected to perform at school and at home. A list of daily and weekly chores will be made for each child, which is to be completed by a certain time. This list may be negotiated, but the final decision of which chores are to be done at what time rests with Mom or Dad.

Schoolwork must be completed appropriately. Because all of you are capable, you are expected to complete 100% of your homework and hand it in on time. Additionally, you are expected to achieve test grades of C and above. And finally, although it should go without saying, you are expected to behave appropriate at school, according to their rules and boundaries.

Section III: What Meeting the Four Expectations Will Earn You

Of course, we should all do what we ought to do out of respect, love, and gratefulness. Our hope is that you will independently develop the self-discipline and drive to meet the Four Expectations. We also recognize that you all desire certain rewards that show Mom and Dad's appreciation, trust, and respect. You may take the opportunity to request certain rewards. Mom and Dad are eager to give you the following Four Rewards for meeting the Four Expectations.

Trust. This refers to

_____

_____

_____

_____

_____

_____

_____

_____

_____

Respect. This refers to

_____

_____

_____

_____

_____

_____

_____

_____

_____

Freedom. This refers to

_____

_____

_____

_____

_____

_____

_____

Privileges. This refers to

_____

_____

_____

_____

_____

_____

_____

Section IV: Rights versus Privileges

It is important that you know what your rights are and what you must earn by meeting the Four Expectations.

No matter what, you have a right to our love. Until you are an adult, we will always take care of your basic needs, including food, clothes, and a safe place to live. Some additional rights are:

_____

_____

_____

_____

_____

_____

_____

_____

_____

In addition to these, Mom and Dad will consider many enjoyable things *privileges*—that is, you must earn them. We sincerely hope that you do earn them; we hope that you have every privilege available to you. But you must earn them. This list will grow and shrink as you grow, but here are some things that are privileges in our home:

_____

_____

_____

_____

_____

_____

_____

_____

_____

Section V: Our Family Values

This family stands for things. It values certain principles and believes certain things.

_____
_____
_____
_____
_____
_____
_____
_____
_____

The following changes will begin on the following date
_____, after an additional family meeting, where all family members will have an opportunity to express their opinions, question, and thoughts about these changes.

We ask you to sign this Constitution, acknowledging that you understand its contents. Your signature does <u>not</u> mean that you agree with all of it—only that you comprehend it.

_____   _____
_____   _____
_____   _____

Date: _____

Appendix B
Top Ten Behaviors that Parents in Charge <u>Never</u> Tolerate

Remember, **Parents in Charge** do not have perfect children. Their children break rules and can be foolish, selfish, and plain ridiculous just like any other children. However, Parents in Charge respond appropriately and do not tolerate any disrespect. They expect their children to exhibit superb behavior and reinforce them when they behave well. When their cherubs choose to misbehave, they lovingly but firmly enforce consequences that make them wish they had behaved better.

The following is a list of behaviors I see many parents tolerating that simply should not be.

1. **Parents in Charge** do not allow their children to order them in any way: not about meals, not about wheels, not about stations, not about vacations. They will not boss them here or there; they will not boss them anywhere!

2. Children who have **Parents in Charge** do not *Answer Shop* (e.g., appeal to Dad when Mom has said "no") because they know they will be arrested for shoplifting.

3. **Parents in Charge** do not tolerate eye-rolling, arm-folding, stomping, door-slamming, or any looks that suggest they are from another planet, especially when establishing limits or bestowing one of their many invaluable pearls of wisdom.

4. **Parents in Charge** do not tolerate children whispering "whatever" or speaking anything under their breath to or about them.

5. **Parents in Charge** do not sustain their child's whining, nagging, or even adorable begging in order to get things that should be gotten with "Please, may I…" **Parents in Charge** can spot and dodge even the best brown-nosing maneuvers.

6. Insulting a **Parent in Charge** never pays because **Parents in Charge** never tolerate their child calling them "retarded",

"lame", or "backward" (even though all parents slip and might indeed be lame or backward from time to time).

7. **Parents in Charge** do not suffer complaints of boredom. They respond to such complaints by saying, "Only boring people get bored. Interesting people find or create something to do. If you would like my guidance, I have a fantastic list of chores that could keep you occupied for hours. Would you…hey, where are you going?!"

8. In restaurants, **Parents in Charge** do not tolerate obnoxious behavior. If their child acts out, they take him outside or to the bathroom, establish the seriousness of the expectations, give him an attitude adjustment if necessary, and assure him that if he acts out again, he will be eating wheat bread and broccoli when he gets home. **Parents in Charge** follow through with this.

9. **Parents in Charge** never tolerate other children misbehaving in their home without consequence. Rather, a **Parent in Charge** asserts his sovereignty gently but firmly, confronting any misbehavior and removing the child from the home if necessary. Afterwards, the parent communicates very clearly to that child's parents what occurred and which behaviors will not be tolerated in their home. Finally, the **Parent in Charge** extends an open invitation for the child to return to the home *if* the child can respect the family's limits and boundaries.

10. Finally, **Parents in Charge** witness no positive behavior from their children without frequently acknowledging, appreciating, praising, respecting, or expressing gratitude for it. **Parents in Charge** know their children crave their love, acceptance, attention, and approval and waste no opportunity to dole it out.

Appendix C
Grade Cards

Child:_____ Week of:_____

Expectations:	Safety	Respect	Obedience	Work
Grade:				
Notes:				

Parents:_____ Week of:_____

Rewards:	Respect	Trust	Freedom	Privileges
Grade:				
Notes:				

Bibliography

Subject

ADD/ADHD/Learning Disabilities

Armstrong, T. (1997). *The Myth of ADD: 50 Ways to Improve Your Child's Behavior and Attention Span Without Drugs, Labels, or Coercion*. New York: Plume.

Baughman, F. (2006). *The ADHD Fraud: How Psychiatry Makes "Patients" Out of Normal Children*. Bloomington: Trafford.

Haber, J. (2000). *ADHD: The Great Misdiagnosis. Dallas*: Taylor.

Stein, D. (2001). *Unraveling the ADD/ADHD Fiasco*. Kansas City: Andrews NcNeel.
Stein, D. (1999). *Ritalin is not the Answer*. San Francisco: Jossey-Bass.

Diagnosis

Ravenel, B., Rosemond, J. (2008). *The Diseasing of America's Children*. Nashville: Thomas Nelson.

Discipline

Easley, J., Glasser, H. (1999). *Transforming the Difficult Child: The Nurtured Heart Approach*. Nurtured Heart Publications.

Johnson, M. (2001). *Positive Parenting with a Plan*. Publication Consultants.

Leman, K. (2008). *Have a New Kid By Friday*. Grand Rapids: Revell.

General Parenting

Boteach, S. (2003). *Judaism for Everyone: Renewing Your Life Through the Vibrant Lessons of the Jewish Faith*. New York: Basic Books.

Mellor, C. (2004). *The Three-Martini Playdate: A Practical Guide to Happy Parenting*. San Francisco: Chronicle Books.

Owens, J., Mindell, J. (2005). *Take Charge of Your Child's Sleep*. New York: Marlowe & Company.

Wilkoff, W. (2000). *Is My Child Overtired?* NY: Fireside.

Internet Safety

Miller Cindrich, S. (2007). *e-parenting: Keeping up With Your Tech-Savvy Kids*. NY: Random House.

Smith, G. (2007). *How to Protect Your Children on the Internet: A Road Map for Parents and Teachers*. Westport: Praeger.

Psychiatric Medications

Breggin, P. (2002). *The Ritalin Fact Book: What your Doctor Won't Tell You About ADHD and Stimulant Drugs*. Cambridge: De Capo Press.

Breggin, P. (1997). *Talking Back to Ritalin*. Cambridge: De Capo Press.

School Issues

Breggin, P. (2000). *Reclaiming Our Children: A Healing Plan for a Nation in Crisis*. Cambridge: Perseus.

Rosemond, J. (1990). *Ending the Homework Hassle*. Kansas City: Andrews McNeel.

Toilet Training

Mack, A. (1990). *Dry All Night: The Picture-Book Technique that Stops Bedwetting*. UK: Little, Brown.

About the Author

Dr. Dathan Paterno is a Licensed Clinical Psychologist who has been working with children and families for more than 18 years. Since 2006, he has been Clinical Director of Park Ridge Psychological Services, a private practice in Northwest Chicago dedicated to holistic treatment of emotional, behavioral, and psychological struggles.

Before receiving his Doctor of Psychology at the Illinois School of Professional Psychology, Chicago, he worked with children in a variety of settings, including psychiatric hospitals, residential treatment centers, and a therapeutic day school. He developed an adjunct journal therapy workbook for children and adolescents entitled *The Take Home Therapist*, which continues to be used in several inpatient settings.

Dr. Paterno is also an Executive Board Member and Senior Researcher at the *International Center for the Study of Psychology and Psychiatry*. He currently consults with the Chicago Archdiocese in developing school behavioral programs and bullying policies. He has also taught Psychology at William Rainey Harper College.

In his free time, he enjoys gardening, playing volleyball, reading, showing no mercy to his eldest daughter in Boggle, pretending to like *Barbie on Ice*, teaching his son how to air guitar to Led Zeppelin, and trying to practice what he preaches with all of his wonderful and appropriately obnoxious children.

Dr. Paterno maintains a parenting blog consistent with the ideas in this book, called *Desperately Seeking Parents*. Found at www.drpaterno. blogspot.com, all are welcome to read and comment on the posts, as well as suggest ideas for new posts.